# Best Easy Day Hikes
# Boulder

## Help Us Keep This Guide Up to Date

Every effort has been made by the author and editors to make this guide as accurate and useful as possible. However, many things can change after a guide is published—trails are rerouted, regulations change, facilities come under new management, etc.

We would appreciate hearing from you concerning your experiences with this guide and how you feel it could be improved and kept up to date. While we may not be able to respond to all comments and suggestions, we'll take them to heart and we'll also make certain to share them with the author. Please send your comments and suggestions to the following address:

> GPP
> Reader Response/Editorial Department
> P.O. Box 480
> Guilford, CT 06437

Or you may e-mail us at:

> editorial@GlobePequot.com

Thanks for your input, and happy trails!

Best Easy Day Hikes Series

# Best Easy Day Hikes
# Boulder

Second Edition

**Tracy Salcedo-Chourré**

GUILFORD, CONNECTICUT
HELENA, MONTANA
AN IMPRINT OF GLOBE PEQUOT PRESS

# FALCONGUIDES®

Copyright © 2011 by Morris Book Publishing, LLC

FalconGuides is an imprint of Globe Pequot Press.

Falcon, FalconGuides, and Outfit Your Mind are registered trademarks of Morris Book Publishing, LLC.

TOPO! Explorer software and SuperQuad source maps courtesy of National Geographic Maps. For information about TOPO! Explorer, TOPO!, and Nat Geo Maps products, go to www.topo.com or www.natgeomaps.com.

Project editor: David Legere
Layout artist: Kevin Mak

Maps created by Bruce Grubbs © Morris Book Publishing, LLC

Library of Congress Cataloging-in-Publication Data is available on file.

ISBN 978-0-7627-6103-6

Printed in the United States of America
10 9 8 7 6 5 4 3 2 1

# Contents

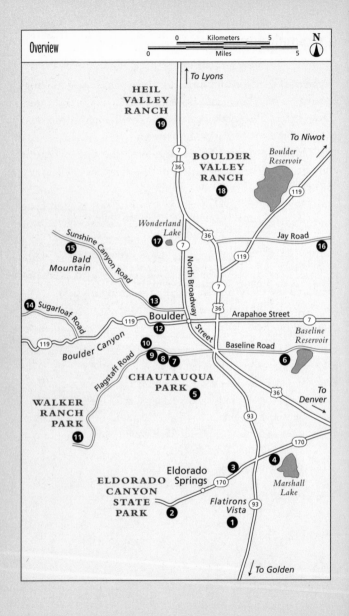

# Acknowledgments

Thanks to these organizations for their help reviewing hike descriptions for accuracy: Boulder County Parks and Open Space; City of Boulder Open Space & Mountain Parks; and the Colorado State Parks Department.

Thanks to these folks for help with the first edition of this guide: Pascale Fried, Brent Wheeler, Matt Claussen, George Meyers, and Erica Olsen.

Thanks to the expert editors, layout artists, mapmakers, and proofreaders at FalconGuides and Globe Pequot Press for making this guide the best it can be.

Thanks to Karen Charland, Peggy Biehoffer, and Penn Chourré for company on the trails. Thanks to the Salcedo clan and the Chourré clan for their ongoing support.

Most of all, thanks to my sons, Jesse, Cruz, and Penn; and my husband, Martin.

# Introduction

The Flatirons, distinctive slabs of smooth red rock, bridge the gap between the city of Boulder and Colorado's high country. The rocks are a defining feature of the college town's landscape, and their skyward reach beckons hikers, climbers, and skiers onto higher ground.

Like the Flatirons, Boulder is unique. It boasts the hippest people, food, and shopping in the state; the educational stimulus of the University of Colorado's flagship campus; and some of the Front Range's loveliest terrain. It's also a recreational mecca: Hiking is just one selection in a candy store of outdoor activities you can choose from. With this collection of trails, I've tried to pay suitable homage to Boulder's spirit and landscape. Many of the hikes are in sight of the Flatirons' stunning natural architecture; the rest explore the high country to the west, and a few venture onto the prairie that stretches eastward.

This guide has been a long time in the making, having its origins in a *12 Short Hikes* guide I wrote more than fifteen years ago, just after my twins were born. The first Falcon edition was an expansion of that guide; this is a distillation of both, with updated information on old favorites and a few new routes. To accommodate the new, I've had to jettison some of the old, but I've retained references to those hikes as options. Parting with the oldies was hard, but Boulder is blessed in its dedication to the preservation and sustainable use of its wildlands, so endless possibilities for future modification—and for exploration—remain.

I've been away from the Rockies for a few years now. But, having spent seventeen years of my adult life in Colorado, it is and always will be my second home. In researching trails for this second edition, I was struck yet again by the grandeur of Boulder's landscape and felt fortunate to be able to walk old, familiar paths with a new, more appreciative perspective. I hope this guidebook will not only get you out there but will also inspire you to support the ongoing preservation efforts that have been so successful through years. Hike on!

## The Nature of Boulder

Trails in Boulder and its foothills range from rough and hilly to flat and paved. Hikes in this guide cover the gamut. While by definition a best easy day hike poses little danger to the traveler, knowing a few details about the nature of the region will enhance your explorations.

### Weather
Late spring, summer, and fall are the optimal times to enjoy trails on Colorado's Front Range. Temperatures are generally moderate, and precipitation is usually limited to scattered afternoon thunderstorms.

Typical daytime temperatures in the prime hiking season range from the mid-50s to the upper 80s, with the occasional heat wave or cold snap. Generally, the higher you go in elevation, the cooler the air, so if hot weather is predicted for the plains, venture into the high country for cooler temps.

Thunderstorms are most likely early in spring and in late summer, when monsoon moisture from the south collides with cooler mountain air to create dangerous thunderheads. To avoid the potential hazards of lightning strikes and heavy rain, try to be off the trail by midafternoon. Be sure to wear layers and carry rain gear.

Winter cold, snow, and ice may limit access to trails between October and May, but with the proper gear, especially waterproof footwear, many of the routes described herein can be traveled year-round.

**Potential Hazards**

While the only critters you're likely to encounter on Boulder's trails are butterflies and bunnies, there is the chance you may run across an animal with the potential to cause harm.

Encounters with bears, rattlesnakes, and mountain lions are unlikely, but possible. Signs at trailheads warn hikers if these animals might be present and in most cases include information on how you should behave in the event of an encounter. Making noise while hiking will likely scare off any black bears in the vicinity. Snakes generally only strike if they are threatened: Keep your distance, and they will keep theirs. If you come across a cat, make yourself as big as possible—do *not* run. If you don't act like or look like prey, you stand a good chance of not being attacked.

Ticks, potential vectors of Lyme disease and Rocky Mountain spotted fever, also abide in the region. Wear light-colored, long-sleeved shirts and trousers so that you can see the bugs. Remove any ticks that attach as quickly as possible, and seek medical treatment if a rash or illness occurs after a tick bite.

# Be Prepared

Hikers should be prepared for any situation, whether they are out for a short stroll around Walden Ponds Wildlife Habitat or climbing to the summit of Sugarloaf Mountain. Some specific advice:

- Know the basics of first aid, including how to treat bleeding; bites and stings; and fractures, strains, or sprains. Pack a first-aid kit on each excursion.

- Know the symptoms of both cold- and heat-related conditions, including hypothermia and heat stroke. The best way to avoid these afflictions is to wear appropriate clothing, drink lots of water, eat enough to keep the internal fires properly stoked, and keep a pace that is within your physical limits.

- Regardless of the weather, your body needs a lot of water while hiking. Drinking a full thirty-two-ounce bottle on each outing is a good idea, no matter how short the hike. More is better.

- Don't drink from rivers, creeks, or lakes without treating or filtering the water first. Untreated water may host a variety of contaminants, including giardia, which can cause serious intestinal unrest.

- Be prepared for the vagaries of Colorado weather. It changes in a heartbeat. The sun is more intense at elevation, so wear sunscreen. Afternoon and evening thunderstorms harbor a host of potential hazards, including rain, hail, and lightning. Know how to protect yourself. And yes, snow may fall even in summer, so be on guard.

- Carry a backpack in which you can store extra clothing, water, food, and goodies like guidebooks, a camera, and binoculars.

- Some trails have cell phone coverage. Bring your device, but make sure it's turned off or on the vibrate setting so a call won't startle wildlife or other hikers.

- Hike with a partner or group. If that's not possible, leave information about your route and expected duration with a friend or family member.
- Watch children carefully. Waterways move deceptively fast; animals and plants may be dangerous; and steep, rocky terrain poses a potential hazard. Children should carry a plastic whistle: If they become lost, they should stay in one place and blow the whistle to summon help.

## Leave No Trace

Trails in Boulder and its foothills are heavily used year-round. We, as trail users and advocates, must be especially vigilant to ensure our passage leaves no lasting mark. Here are some basic guidelines for preserving trails in the region:

- Pack out all trash, including biodegradable items like apple cores. You might also pack out garbage left by less-considerate hikers.
- Avoid damaging fragile soils and plants by remaining on established routes and not cutting switchbacks. Social trails contribute to erosion problems and create unsightly scars on the landscape.
- Don't approach or feed any wild creatures—they are best able to survive if they remain self-reliant.
- Don't pick wildflowers or gather rocks, antlers, feathers, and other treasures along the trail. Removing these items will only take away from the next hiker's experience.
- Be courteous by not making loud noises while hiking.
- Many of these trails are multiuse, which means you'll share them with other hikers, trail runners, mountain

bikers, and equestrians. Familiarize yourself with the proper trail etiquette, yielding the trail when appropriate. If you are hiking with a group, walk single file when passing other hikers.

- Use outhouses at trailheads or along the trail.

## Dogs

Boulder is one of the few cities on the Front Range that allows dogs to walk off-leash on trails, provided they and their owners have registered in the city's Voice & Sight Dog Tag Program. To enroll in the program, dog owners must watch a training video and certify that their pet will respond to verbal commands regardless of distractions and not display aggressive behavior toward people or other dogs. Dogs walking off-leash on City of Boulder parklands must display the Voice & Sight tag. For more information contact the City of Boulder Open Space and Mountain Parks Department at (303) 441-3440 or visit www.osmp.org.

## Getting Around

All hikes in this guide are within an hour's drive of downtown Boulder. Directions to each trailhead are given from the nearest major highway or from the intersection of Broadway and Baseline Road just south of downtown.

Major thoroughfares include Broadway (CO 93), which runs north–south; Baseline and Flagstaff Roads, which run east–west; US 36 (28th Street), which runs north–south; and CO 119 (Boulder Canyon Drive/Canyon Boulevard), which runs east–west.

Public transportation generally doesn't run directly to trailheads but can get you close. Contact the Regional

Transport District (RTD) at (303) 299-6000 or (800) 366-RIDE (7433) or visit www.rtd-denver.com for more information. The Boulder Transit Center is at 1400 Walnut St. in downtown Boulder; call (303) 442-7332.

## Land Management

The following government agencies manage public lands described in this guide and can provide further information on other trails and parks in their service areas.

- City of Boulder Open Space & Mountain Parks, P.O. Box 791, Boulder, CO 80306; (303) 441-3440; www .osmp.org
- Boulder County Parks and Open Space, 5201 St. Vrain Rd., Longmont, CO 80503; (303) 678-6200; www .bouldercounty.org/openspace
- Colorado State Parks, 1313 Sherman St., Suite 618, Denver, CO 80203; (303) 866-3437; www.parks.state .co.us

# How to Use This Guide

This guide is designed to be simple and easy to use. Each hike is described with a map and summary information that delivers the trail's vital statistics including length, difficulty, fees and permits, park hours, canine compatibility, and trail contact. Directions to the trailhead are provided. Information about what you'll see along each trail, as well as tidbits about natural and cultural history, are included in hike descriptions. A detailed route finder (Miles and Directions) sets forth mileages between significant landmarks.

## How the Hikes Were Chosen

Hikes range in difficulty from flat excursions in urban settings to more challenging treks in the foothills. I've selected hikes in a variety of settings in different parts of town, so wherever your starting point, you'll find an easy day hike nearby.

While these trails are among the best, keep in mind that nearby trails or parks may offer options better suited to your needs. Potential alternatives, including omitted routes from the first edition of this guide, are suggested in the Options section at the end of some hike descriptions.

## Selecting a Hike

These are all easy hikes, but *easy* is a relative term. Some would argue that no hike involving any kind of climbing is easy, but in Boulder, hills are a fact of life. To aid in selecting a hike that suits particular needs and abilities, hikes are rated easy, moderate, and more challenging. Bear in mind that even the most challenging can be made easy by hiking within your limits and taking rests when you need them.

- **Easy** hikes are generally short and flat, taking no longer than an hour to complete.
- **Moderate** hikes involve increased distance and changes in elevation and take one to two hours to complete.
- **More challenging** hikes feature some steep stretches and generally take longer than two hours to complete.

What you think is easy is entirely dependent on your level of fitness and the adequacy of your gear (primarily shoes). Use the trail's length as a gauge of its relative difficulty—even if climbing is involved, it won't be bad if the hike is less than 1 mile long. If you are hiking with a group, select a hike that's appropriate for the least fit and prepared in your party.

Approximate hiking times are based on the assumption that on flat ground, most walkers average 2 miles per hour. Adjust that rate by the steepness of the terrain and your level of fitness (subtract time if you're an aerobic animal and add time if you're hiking with kids). Be sure to add time if you plan to picnic or take part in other activities like birding or photography.

# Trail Finder

**Best Hikes for Great Views**

**Best Hikes for Nature Lovers**

**Best Hikes for History Lovers**

**Best Hikes Near Lakes or Streams**

**Best Hikes with Children**

**Best Hikes with Dogs**

## Best Hikes for a Workout

## Hike Ratings

*(Hikes are listed from easiest to most challenging.)*

# Map Legend

| | |
|---|---|
| ═══⟨36⟩═══ | U.S. Highway |
| ───⟨7⟩─── | State Highway |
| ─────── | Local Road |
| = = = = = = | Unpaved Road |
| ⊢ ─ ─ ─ ─ ⊣ | Tunnel |
| ▬▬▬▬▬▬ | Featured Trail |
| - - - - - - - | Trail |
| ━━━━━━ | Paved/Bike Trail |
| ⊢+++++⊣ | Railroad |
| ⬭ | Body of Water |
| ∼∼∼∼ | River/Creek |
| ─··─··─ | Intermittent stream |
| ⟿ | Marsh |
| ⣏⣹ | State or Local Park/Preserve |
| ‖‖‖‖‖‖‖ | Boardwalk |
| ⌣ | Bridge |
| •─• | Gate |
| ▲ | Mountain Peak |
| 🅿 | Parking |
| 🛆 | Picnic Area |
| ▪ | Point of Interest/Structure |
| 🚻 | Restroom |
| ○ | Town |
| ❶ | Trailhead |
| 🔭 | Viewpoint/Overlook |
| ❓ | Visitor/Information Center |

# 1 Flatirons Vista Loop

Boulder's famous Flatirons form the backdrop for this mesa-top ramble, with open prairie views spreading east on the downhill side.

**Distance:** 2.4-mile lollipop
**Approximate hiking time:** 1.5 hours
**Difficulty:** Easy
**Trail surface:** Dirt access road, dirt trail
**Best seasons:** Spring through fall
**Other trail users:** Mountain bikers, equestrians
**Canine compatibility:** Leashed dogs permitted; dogs permitted off-leash if displaying a Boulder Voice & Sight dog tag. Dogs must be on leash in the parking area and on the lower Towhee Trail.

**Fees and permits:** No fees or permits required
**Schedule:** Sunrise to sunset daily
**Trailhead facilities:** Large parking area, restrooms, trash cans, information signboard
**Maps:** USGS Louisville
**Other:** The Prairie Vista Trail is wheelchair accessible and interpretive.
**Trail contacts:** City of Boulder Open Space & Mountain Parks, P.O. Box 791, Boulder, CO 80306; (303) 441-3440; www.osmp.org

**Finding the trailhead:** From the intersection of Baseline Road and Broadway (1 block west of the junction of US 36 and Baseline), head south on Broadway (CO 93). Follow CO 93 for 6 miles to the signed Flatirons Vista trailhead and parking area on the right (west). GPS: N39 55.429' / W105 14.131'

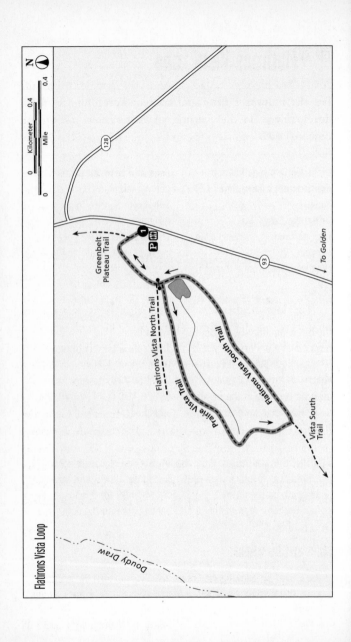

Flatirons Vista Loop

Doudy Draw

Greenbelt Plateau Trail

Flatirons Vista North Trail

Prairie Vista Trail

Flatirons Vista South Trail

Vista South Trail

To Golden

N

Kilometer    0    0.4
Mile         0    0.4

# The Hike

A swath of high prairie just south of the Boulder basin buffers the mountain front and the signature Flatirons from development on the flatlands. A network of hiking and multiuse trails crisscross the grassland, including this lovely little loop.

The trail names say it all. The Prairie Vista Trail meanders through meadows filled with wildflowers in spring and summer; Flatirons Vista offers views of the Flatirons as well as of the high plains. Glimpses of residential areas, power lines, and a concrete processing plant on the south side of CO 93—most obvious on the return leg of the loop—highlight the urban-wildland interface that defines the Front Range.

The loop begins with a gentle climb west toward the mountains on the Prairie Vista Trail. The trail follows a shallow draw that feeds a small pond at its low point. At the head of the draw, the route crosses a couple of streamlets that may dry up toward the end of summer, then tops out among widely spaced ponderosas.

The Flatirons Vista South Trail drops from the top of the draw through the ponderosa (which don't impede the views in the least) back into the open rangeland. Watchful cattle may mark your progress down the track—if they aren't too busy cropping the grass. The tail end of the loop leads across the pond's dam to the start of the loop; from here retrace your steps to the trailhead.

## Miles and Directions

**0.0** Start by following the Prairie Vista Trail up past the informational signboard. A series of trail intersections follows. At the first, about 350 feet up the trail, stay left on the Prairie Vista Trail (the Greenbelt Plateau Trail goes right). About 100 feet farther, stay left on the Prairie Vista/Flatirons Vista North Trail (again avoiding a right turn onto the Greenbelt Plateau route).

**0.3** At the gate, stay left on the Prairie Vista/Flatirons Vista South Trail, down toward the pond. Flatirons Vista North goes straight (west). At the junction about 30 feet downhill, go right on the signed Prairie Vista Trail, passing an interpretive sign. Begin the gentle climb west up the draw.

**1.0** At the head of the draw, cross a pair of streams and begin walking through the sparse ponderosa forest.

**1.25** Reach the junction with the Flatirons Vista South Trail. Go left on Flatirons Vista South.

**2.0** Drop onto the dam of the pond and climb to the junction with the Flatirons Vista North Trail, closing the loop. Turn right and retrace your steps to the trailhead.

**2.4** Arrive back at the trailhead.

### Options

Boulder's Open Space & Mountain Parks (OSMP) program maintains a number of wonderful trail loops in this area. Trails in Doudy Draw climb to the mesa top and connect to the Community Ditch and Flatirons Vista Trails. The Big Bluestem and South Boulder Creek Trails form a nice loop a bit farther north, with the signed trailhead just off CO 93 near Thomas Lane. Pick up a copy of the OSMP map and pick a route that matches your ambition, or try them all.

# 2  Rattlesnake Gulch (Eldorado Canyon State Park)

Follow the old "Crags Boulevard" to the remains of the Crags Hotel, enjoying views of surrounding rock–climbing walls as you ascend and of the Continental Divide from the hotel site.

**Distance:** 2.8 miles out and back

**Approximate hiking time:** 2 hours

**Difficulty:** Moderate due to a 700-foot elevation change

**Trail surface:** Dirt road and singletrack

**Best seasons:** Late spring, summer, and fall

**Other trail users:** Mountain bikers

**Canine compatibility:** Leashed dogs permitted

**Fees and permits:** Entrance fee

**Schedule:** Sunrise to sunset daily

**Trailhead facilities:** Parking for about ten cars and an information signboard at the trailhead; a dozen additional spaces are available 100 yards to the west; restrooms and water available farther up the park road at the visitor center.

**Maps:** USGS Eldorado Springs; Eldorado Canyon State Park brochure

**Special considerations:** Please leave all artifacts in place for the next hiker to enjoy.

**Trail contacts:** Eldorado Canyon State Park, P.O. Box B/9 Kneale Road, Eldorado Springs, CO 80025; (303) 494-3943; parks .state.co.us/parks/eldorado canyon/Pages/EldoradoCanyon Home.aspx

**Finding the trailhead:** From the intersection of Baseline Road and Broadway, follow Broadway (CO 93) south for 4 miles to the stoplight at Eldorado Canyon Road (CO 170). Turn right (west) onto CO

170 and follow it for 3.5 miles to the Eldorado Canyon State Park entrance and fee station. Drive up the park road for about 0.6 mile to the trailhead, on the left (south) side. GPS: N39 55.785' / W105 17.487'

## The Hike

Slowly succumbing to the forces of wind, snow, and sun, a brick oven perched on a spectacular promontory opens onto the ragged rock walls of Eldorado Canyon and the distant Continental Divide. Hikers have collected broken bits of pottery and glass and placed them on the oven's mantle, a shrine to history. The oven, potsherds, the basin of a fountain, and other scattered artifacts are all that remain of the Crags Hotel, for a brief time host to Colorado's wealthy.

The hotel stood on this spot for four years before it was destroyed by fire. Patrons reached the hotel in automobiles via the "boulevard" that now serves as the Rattlesnake Gulch Trail, by taking a funicular rail line, or by riding the Moffat Railroad from Denver ($1 round-trip), then taking a horse-and-buggy ride from the rail stop down to the hotel. An interpretive sign at the site describes the hotel's grandeur and demise. From its perch on the north-facing slope of Eldorado Canyon, modern-day visitors can savor the same scenery that drew visitors a hundred years ago, including views of the snowcapped Indian Peaks and the canyon's famed rock-climbing walls.

The grade of the Rattlesnake Gulch Trail is steady and relatively easy, and with its north-facing aspect, the route is shady and cool even on hot summer days. A visit in the afternoon or evening, when the setting sun stains the cliffs shades of gold, red, and slate, can't be beat.

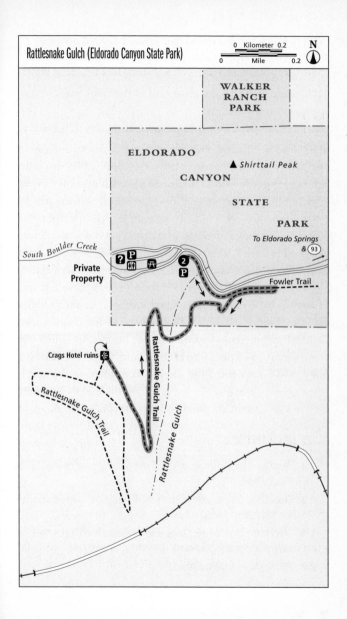

Rattlesnake Gulch (Eldorado Canyon State Park)

0     Kilometer   0.2
0     Mile   0.2

N

WALKER
RANCH
PARK

ELDORADO

▲ Shirttail Peak

CANYON

STATE

PARK

To Eldorado Springs
& 93

South Boulder Creek

Private
Property

?  P
🚻  ⛱

2
P

Fowler Trail

Crags Hotel ruins

Rattlesnake Gulch Trail

Rattlesnake Gulch Trail

Rattlesnake Gulch

To begin, walk east on the broad, gravel Fowler Trail, which parallels the park road and South Boulder Creek. Just as views of the plains appear through the canyon mouth, the Rattlesnake Gulch Trail breaks off to the right, switchbacking uphill into the draw.

The trail climbs past talus slopes that have achieved an angle of repose on either side of the path, then through a flat, grassy area dotted with concrete foundations that are a perfect place to rest. The large concrete pipe at the south end of this area supplies water to Ralston Reservoir on the flatlands. Curve through the back of the gulch and then traverse east-facing slopes, where you will be treated to views of the steep spires and faces that make Eldorado Canyon a rock-climbing mecca. The Denver and Rio Grande Railroad is chiseled into the mountainside above: If a train passes, the rumble of the engines and the otherworldly whine of wheels on rails well up in the ravine.

The interpretive marker and the hotel site mark the turnaround point for this route, with social trails breaking right to explore the ruins. Once you have satisfied your inner archaeologist, return to the trailhead via the same route.

## Miles and Directions

- **0.0** Start by heading left (east) from the parking area on the Fowler Trail.
- **0.3** Reach the Rattlesnake Gulch Trail. Turn right and head uphill on the gently graded track.
- **1.4** Reach the ruins of the Crags Hotel. Explore and then retrace your steps to the trailhead.
- **2.8** Arrive back at the trailhead.

## Options

You can continue on the Rattlesnake Gulch Trail, which makes a 0.8-mile loop through the upper reaches of the gulch. Another great short hike in the park follows the Eldorado Canyon Trail past the park's famous rock-climbing walls and then up to a scenic viewpoint. This trail eventually links to Walker Ranch, a long excursion well outside the parameters of "easy." Continuing down-canyon on the Fowler Trail—outfitted with binoculars and a telescope for bird- and climber-watching—makes a short, easy addition as well.

# 3  Towhee and Homestead Loop

This gentle loop encompasses tumbling South Boulder Creek, the historic Doudy-Debacker-Dunn House, and the interface of evergreen woodland and tallgrass prairie in lower Shadow Canyon.

**Distance:** 2.25-mile loop
**Approximate hiking time:** 2 hours
**Difficulty:** Moderate due to a 360-foot elevation gain
**Trail surface:** Rocky dirt trail
**Best seasons:** Late spring, summer, fall
**Other trail users:** None
**Canine compatibility:** Leashed dogs permitted; dogs permitted off-leash if displaying a Boulder Voice & Sight dog tag. Dogs must be leashed in the parking area and on the lower Towhee Trail.

**Fees and permits:** No fees or permits required
**Schedule:** Sunrise to sunset daily
**Trailhead facilities:** Large parking area, restrooms, picnic tables, trash cans, dog waste station, informational kiosk
**Maps:** USGS Eldorado Springs; Boulder Open Space & Mountain Parks Circle Hikes Guide
**Trail contacts:** City of Boulder Open Space & Mountain Parks, P.O. Box 791, Boulder, CO 80306; (303) 441-3440; www .osmp.org

**Finding the trailhead:** From the intersection of Broadway and Baseline Road, follow Broadway (CO 93) south for 4 miles to Eldorado Canyon Road (CO 170). Turn right (west) onto CO 170 and go 1.5 miles to the South Mesa trailhead parking area, which is on the right (north). GPS: N39 56.314' / W105 15.476'

# The Hike

Beginning and ending on the cottonwood-shaded banks of South Boulder Creek, this loop showcases both the natural and man-made history of the area. The red-rock portals of Eldorado Canyon and the sweep of the Flatirons add a distinctive Boulder twist, but the scenery is dominated by the wildflower-rich tallgrass and mixed-grass prairie that fronts the foothills.

The route begins on the signed Mesa Trail, first crossing a small bridge spanning the Davidson Ditch and then a more substantial wooden bridge over South Boulder Creek. The picturesque Doudy-Debacker-Dunn House—two stories of stone, wood, and homesteading history—stands on the left side of the trail about 100 yards from the creek. The house is named for its three owners, and an interpretive sign details the history of the house and ranch, which was established in 1858 and once included a gristmill and sawmill.

From the homestead, a few turns take you from the Mesa Trail to the Towhee Trail, which you'll follow up and west toward the Flatirons and distinctive Devils Thumb. The trail makes a mostly gentle ascent toward Shadow Canyon, punctuated by occasional steep sections. The surrounding meadows ring with birdsong and are studded with wildflowers and red sandstone boulders. A rustic log staircase leads to an easy streambed crossing and the junction with an unsigned trail. The Towhee Trail then parallels the waterway as it traverses the south-facing slope of the narrowing gulch. The path grows rougher as it climbs into the draw; stairs aid in the ascent.

The first evergreens shade the trail as you approach the Towhee and Homestead Trail intersection. Turn left

# Towhee and Homestead Loop

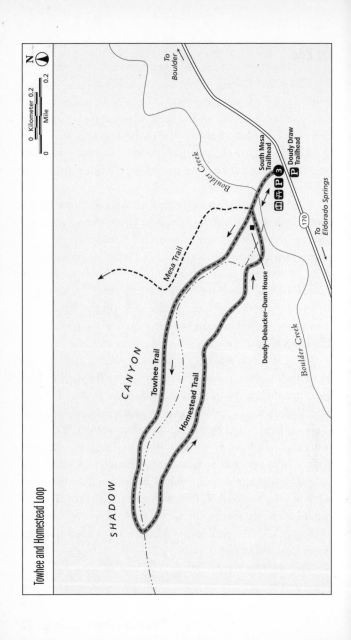

(southeast) on the Homestead Trail, cross the creek, and begin the return leg of the loop.

Climb to a pine-dotted ridgetop before the descent begins, with views of the high plains opening to the east. The trail follows the mesa top down through alternating meadows and glades. Log steps break up the rocky descent. A winding rock-and-log staircase then dives south off the mesa toward the trailhead along Eldorado Canyon Road.

Back on the flats, the Homestead Trail ends at the historic home; pick up the Mesa Trail and retrace your steps back to the trailhead.

## Miles and Directions

**0.0** Start on the Mesa Trail, crossing the bridges over the Davidson Ditch and South Boulder Creek. Ignore side trails branching into the riparian zone along the shores of South Boulder Creek.

**0.1** At the junction of the Mesa and Towhee Trails at the historic house, turn left onto the Towhee Trail; walk about 50 yards, then turn right (northwest) on the Towhee Trail. Dogs must be leashed on this portion of the trail.

**0.5** Drop into the gully and cross a seasonal stream. At the unsigned trail junction, stay straight on the wider path.

**0.8** At the next junction with an unmarked side trail, stay straight on the Towhee Trail.

**1.1** Reach the intersection of the Homestead and Towhee Trails. Turn left onto the Homestead Trail, crossing the creek.

**2.1** At the trail junction, go left on the gravel path toward the Doudy-Debacker-Dunn House. The leg to the right leads to a bench overlooking the creek. Pick up the Mesa Trail on the other side of the house and go right, retracing your steps to the trailhead.

**2.25** Arrive back at the trailhead.

# 4 Marshall Mesa Loop

Once the site of extensive coal mining activity, Marshall Mesa now harbors prairie grasses (and prairie dog colonies), wildflowers, a nice loop hike, and great Flatiron views.

**Distance:** 2.75-mile loop
**Approximate hiking time:** 1.5 hours
**Difficulty:** Easy, with an elevation gain of 180 feet
**Trail surface:** Dirt road and trail
**Best seasons:** Spring, summer, and fall
**Other trail users:** Mountain bikers and equestrians on all but the first segment of the trail loop; no mountain bikes permitted on the Marshall Mesa Trail
**Canine compatibility:** Leashed dogs permitted; dogs permitted off-leash if displaying a Boulder Voice & Sight dog tag

**Fees and permits:** No fees or permits required
**Schedule:** Sunrise to sunset daily
**Trailhead facilities:** Large parking lot, restrooms, trash cans, dog waste station, picnic tables, information kiosk with trail maps
**Maps:** USGS Louisville; Boulder Open Space & Mountain Parks Circle Hikes Guide; Marshall Mesa Trails Guide
**Trail contacts:** City of Boulder Open Space & Mountain Parks, P.O. Box 791, Boulder, CO 80306; (303) 441-3440; www .osmp.org

**Finding the trailhead:** From the intersection of Baseline Road and Broadway, travel 3.7 miles south on Broadway (CO 93) to Marshall Road (CO 170). Turn left (east) onto Marshall Road. The well-signed trailhead and parking area are on the immediate right. GPS: N39 57.171' / W105 13.873'

# The Hike

For nearly eighty years, beginning in the mid-1800s, Marshall Mesa was the site of a huge coal mining operation. Walking through the peaceful prairie that thrives on the mesa today, such activity is difficult to imagine. But traces of the mines remain, and interpretive signs along the trail describe the history—and the controversy—of the mining operations.

The mesa trail loop is pleasant and easy, winding up through blooming grasslands to the Community Ditch and then back down to the trailhead. Views spread north and west to the Flatirons but are curtailed to the east by the undulations of the high plains. Prairie dogs have built an extensive town around the first segment on the trail, in Marshall Valley; the chirping critters stretch up on their hind legs to warn hikers and their dogs to keep their distance. Much of the trail is shared with mountain bikers, so be aware of, and courteous to, these other trail users.

The route begins on a segment of wheelchair-accessible trail, which leads quickly to the junction of the Marshall Valley and Coal Seam Trails. Heading east on the Marshall Valley Trail, the route skirts the prairie dog town on the left and is sparsely shaded by scraggly pines. Pass the junction with a closed trail to the old trailhead (also closed), cross the ditch, and pick up the hikers-only Marshall Mesa Trail, which climbs toward the mesa top. The nice, uphill traverse through meadow, sparse ponderosa, and skunkbrush offers great Flatiron views.

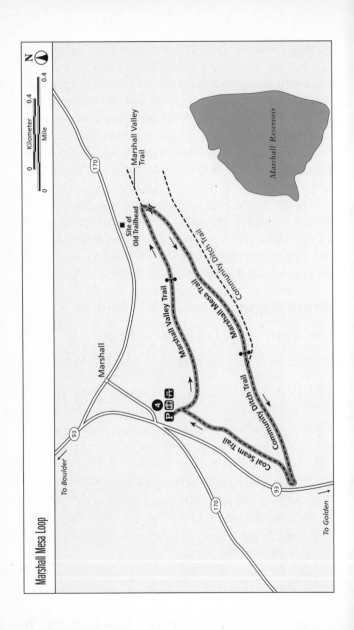

Marshall Mesa Loop

Pass a stained sandstone cliff, where an interpretive sign discusses the GEOLOGY OF A COAL FIELD. In a sloping meadow above, at the junction with a social trail, another interpretive sign describes the underground coal fires that plagued the area. Continue straight (south) on the main trail.

Meet the Community Ditch Trail—a long, flat, multiuse run alongside the ditch itself—beyond the gate at the crest of the Marshall Mesa Trail. Go right (west) on the Community Ditch Trail. Views of the foothills accompany you to the junction with the Coal Seam Trail, just above CO 93 (expect road noise). The Coal Seam Trail leads down into prairie dog territory again, then back to the junction with the wheelchair-accessible trail and the trailhead.

## Miles and Directions

**0.0** Start on the gravel and timber-bordered wheelchair-accessible trail. At the junction with the Marshall Valley and Coal Seam Trails, go left on the Marshall Valley Trail.

**0.5** Pass through the gate.

**0.8** At the junction with the trail to the closed trailhead, stay right on the signed Marshall Valley Trail.

**0.9** Cross a bridge to the junction with the Community Ditch and Marshall Mesa Trails. Continue on the hikers-only Marshall Mesa Trail.

**1.1** Pass the sandstone cliff and interpretive sign.

**1.3** Pass a second interpretive sign at a social trail; stay left on the Marshall Mesa Trail.

**1.6** Pass the gate to the Community Ditch Trail. Go right (west) on the ditch trail.

**1.75** At the junction with the Greenbelt Plateau Trail, stay right on the Community Ditch Trail.

**2.1** At the intersection near CO 93, go right on the Coal Seam Trail.

**2.5** Pass another gate, and cross a bridge over the lower ditch.

**2.6** Close the loop at the junction with the wheelchair-accessible trail. Turn left.

**2.75** Arrive back at the trailhead.

# 5  Walter Orr Roberts Weather Trail

This sweet little loop boasts wonderful interpretive signs and gorgeous views, making it a great option for families with young children and anyone interested in the weather that affects the Front Range.

**Distance:** 0.4-mile figure-eight loop

**Approximate hiking time:** 30 minutes

**Difficulty:** Easy

**Trail surface:** Crushed gravel

**Best seasons:** Year-round

**Other trail users:** None

**Canine compatibility:** Leashed dogs permitted

**Fees and permits:** No fees or permits required

**Schedule:** Sunrise to sunset daily

**Trailhead facilities:** Ample parking in the National Center for Atmospheric Research (NCAR) parking lot; restrooms and water available in the research center

**Maps:** USGS Eldorado Springs

**Special considerations:** The trail is wheelchair accessible.

**Other:** NCAR offers tours of its Mesa Laboratory facility, and displays of weather phenomena enliven its visitor center. The center is open to the public on weekdays from 8 a.m. to 5 p.m. and on weekends and holidays from 9 a.m. to 4 p.m.

**Trail contacts:** National Center for Atmospheric Research, P.O. Box 3000, Boulder, CO 80307-3000; (303) 497-1000; www .ucar.edu/educ_outreach/visit

**Finding the trailhead:** From the intersection of Broadway and Baseline Road, head south on Broadway (CO 93) for 1.2 miles to Table Mesa Drive. Turn right (west) onto Table Mesa Drive and go 2.4 miles to where the road ends in the NCAR parking lot. The trailhead is on the northwest side of the building. You can also reach the trailhead through the visitor center by exiting through the double doors

near the Damon Room, on the second floor above the cafeteria. GPS
(NCAR parking lot): N39 58.781' / W105 16.430'

# The Hike

The wheelchair-accessible Walter Orr Roberts Weather
Trail is the perfect introduction to foothills hiking for visitors to the area. For those who need more distance, the trail
links to the Mesa Trail and the wonderful trail system that
branches off from this artery.

A number of viewpoints with interpretive signs line the
figure-eight path. The signs describe the sometimes fierce
and always interesting weather along the Front Range,
including Denver's infamous "Brown Cloud," chinook
winds, snow, flooding, and thunderstorms. NCAR and
the trail perch on a ridge overlooking Bear Canyon, which
drops steeply to the south. To the east, beyond the striking
architecture of the NCAR building, the high plains present a panorama that shimmers with the silver of development and the gold and green of prairie grasses. To the west
rise the Flatirons, which reach back to the high peaks of
the Continental Divide, where much of the weather that
sweeps over Boulder develops.

You can configure a walk on the figure-eight interpretive trail in any combination you choose. Broad and well
signed, the path winds uphill to the west for about 0.2 mile,
to the junction with the Mesa Trail and access to Boulder's
extensive foothill trail system, then loops back to the trailhead. Several benches are provided for rest and contemplation. An intersecting path runs between the two main arms
of the trail, creating the figure eight.

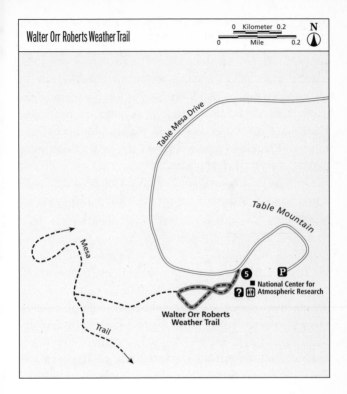

Walter Orr Roberts Weather Trail

National Center for Atmospheric Research

Walter Orr Roberts Weather Trail

## Miles and Directions

**0.0**  Begin on the northwest side of the NCAR building or by exiting the double doors near the Damon Room in the NCAR visitor center and following the ramp to the trail.

**0.2**  Reach the west end of the loop.

**0.4**  Complete the loop at the trailhead on the northwest side of the NCAR building.

## Options

Be sure to visit NCAR's Mesa Laboratory visitor center either before or after your hike. The two floors of educational displays and exhibits are well worth checking out.

You can link to the Mesa Trail at the west end of the nature trail. The Mesa Trail reaches north to the iconic Flatirons, Chautauqua Park, and Flagstaff Mountain, and south to Eldorado Canyon. Or you can go west into more difficult terrain, with the Mallory Cave Trail and the summit of Bear Peak among your options. Pick up the Boulder Open Space & Mountain Parks *Circle Hikes Guide* to see the possibilities.

# 6 South Boulder Creek: Bobolink Nature Trail

Sparkling under a bower of stately cottonwoods, South Boulder Creek is the focus of this pleasant flatland hike.

**Distance:** 2.6 miles out and back

**Approximate hiking time:** 1.5 hours

**Difficulty:** Easy

**Trail surface:** Wheelchair-accessible gravel trail, paved trail

**Best seasons:** Year-round

**Other trail users:** Cyclists, trail runners

**Canine compatibility:** Leashed dogs permitted on the nature trail; dogs permitted off-leash on the South Boulder Creek Trail if displaying a Boulder Voice & Sight dog tag

**Fees and permits:** No fees or permits required

**Schedule:** Sunrise to sunset daily

**Trailhead facilities:** Large gravel parking area, trash cans, picnic sites, dog waste station, information kiosk

**Maps:** USGS Louisville; map available online at www.osmp.org

**Trail contacts:** City of Boulder Open Space & Mountain Parks, P.O. Box 791, Boulder, CO 80306; (303) 441-3440; www.osmp.org

**Finding the trailhead:** From the intersection of Baseline Road and Broadway (CO 93), follow Baseline Road east for 2.6 miles to the trailhead parking area, on the right (south) side of the road about 100 yards west of the intersection of Baseline and Cherryvale Roads. GPS: N39 59.995' / W105 12.903'

# The Hike

The Bobolink Nature Trail section of this easy romp along South Boulder Creek is named for an elusive songbird with distinctive male plumage that includes a yellow cap on the back of his head. While it's not likely you'll see the bird, hiking through its habitat of prairie grasses and riparian shrubs makes for a pleasant outing.

Interpretive signs on the nature trail describe the diversity found along the route. With suburbia encroaching on all sides, the existence of rare plants and animals in this strip of wildland, and the robust health of the ecosystems it supports, has resulted in its designation as a protected natural area by the state of Colorado.

The accessible and well-maintained nature trail is popular with hikers, trail runners, people in wheelchairs, and dog walkers. Streamside benches and small beaches are great for contemplating the shimmering water and the mountain backdrop, which is screened by cottonwoods.

The nature trail ends just beyond a diversion dam on South Boulder Creek, hitching up with the paved South Boulder Creek multiuse path, which has run parallel but out of sight to the east. At the junction a separate paved path heads west, across a bridge, into a neighborhood. The side-by-side trail setup recognizes that cycling is not necessarily compatible with the wildland habitat protected along the creek.

The rest of the trip follows the wide paved trail, where hikers and cyclists comfortably share the ample track. The trail meanders through the transition zone between the prairie and riparian habitats, passing an old, weathered barn. Highway noise from South Boulder Road begins to intrude

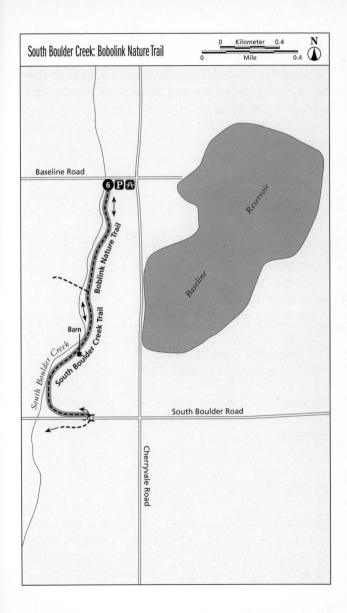

South Boulder Creek: Bobolink Nature Trail

0    Kilometer    0.4

0    Mile    0.4

N

Baseline Road

6 P A

Reservoir

Bobolink Nature Trail

Baseline

South Boulder Creek Trail

Barn

South Boulder Creek

South Boulder Road

Cherryvale Road

as you near trail's end, where you will cross a culvert and then a bridge over a ditch.

A brief stretch of trail runs parallel to the roadway. Cross the creek and reach the tunnel under the road at 1.3 miles; this is the turnaround point (though the culvert and ditch crossing work well too). From the tunnel, retrace your steps to the trailhead.

## Miles and Directions

**0.0** Start at the information kiosk, heading south along the signed gravel nature trail.

**0.5** Reach the end of the nature trail and hook up with the paved South Boulder Creek Trail. A paved neighborhood link goes right, across the bridge. Stay left on the South Boulder Creek Trail.

**0.8** Pass the old barn.

**1.0** Cross the culvert.

**1.3** Pass through the tunnel under South Boulder Road; turn around and retrace your steps.

**2.6** Arrive back at the trailhead.

### Options

The trail continues south to Marshall Road. Dogs are prohibited on this section of trail.

# 7 Enchanted Mesa and McClintock Nature Trails

This easy, well–maintained loop meanders through a lovely woodland, features great views of the high plains and the famous Flatirons, and finishes with a short section through a rich riparian zone.

**Distance:** 2.1-mile loop
**Approximate hiking time:** 1.5 hours
**Difficulty:** Easy, with a 440-foot elevation gain
**Trail surface:** Dirt access road, dirt trail
**Best seasons:** Spring through fall
**Other trail users:** None
**Canine compatibility:** Dogs permitted off-leash if displaying a Boulder Voice & Sight dog tag. Dogs must be leashed in the parking area, on the Enchanted Mesa Trail to the junction at the bridge, and on the upper McClintock Nature Trail.

**Fees and permits:** No fees or permits required
**Schedule:** Sunrise to sunset daily
**Trailhead facilities:** Limited parking at the trailhead, with more parking available on the north side of the auditorium; trash cans, dog waste station, picnic facilities, information kiosk
**Maps:** USGS Eldorado Springs; Boulder Open Space & Mountain Parks Circle Hikes Guide
**Trail contacts:** City of Boulder Open Space & Mountain Parks, P.O. Box 791, Boulder, CO 80306; (303) 441-3440; www.osmp.org

**Finding the trailhead:** From the intersection of Broadway (CO 93) and Baseline Road, go west on Baseline Road for 0.8 mile to 12th Street. Turn left (south) onto 12th Street and follow the road around to the right for 0.3 mile to the Chautauqua Auditorium. A small lot is on the south side of the auditorium; if that is full, park in the larger lot on the north side of the historic building. The trail begins on the southeast side of the auditorium. GPS: N39 59.844' / W105 16.817'

## The Hike

Chautauqua Park, a historic district that backs up to open space lands including the Flatirons and Green Mountain, has been a recreational focal point in Boulder since it opened in 1898. Part of the Chautauqua Movement, according to Colorado Chautauqua Association, the Boulder campus has combined summer camp and summer school since its inception, coupling lectures and classes with concerts and theater—and of course outdoor exploration. The area is now a National Historic Landmark.

The Enchanted Mesa and McClintock Trail loop is ideal for exploring Chautauqua's parklands, given its short length and relatively easy inclines (spiced with a few steep sections, both up and down). The loop tours a woodland with widely spaced trees and filtered views of the Flatirons, then descends via a traverse through Bluebell Canyon. The final stretch is along the quiet stream, rich with wildflowers and shade in spring and summer.

Start by climbing the service road that serves as the Enchanted Mesa Trail, which leads south toward the Flatirons. The walk-and-talk trail climbs gently, with views of Boulder's eastern suburbs and trophy homes. Pass a covered reservoir as the trail bends west toward the mountain front and then meanders lazily through an open pine woodland.

The intersection of the Enchanted Mesa and Mesa Trails is the high point of the loop and a perfect place to take a break. Go ahead, have that candy bar. Then go right (north) on the Mesa Trail, which begins a gentle descent through the forest. When the Mesa Trail intersects the McClintock

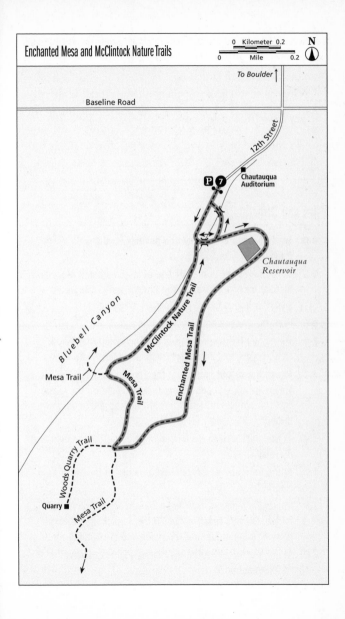

0        Kilometer        0.2

0            Mile            0.2

N

To Boulder ↑

Baseline Road

12th Street

P 7

Chautauqua
Auditorium

Chautauqua
Reservoir

B l u e b e l l   C a n y o n

McClintock Nature Trail

Enchanted Mesa Trail

Mesa Trail

Mesa Trail

Woods Quarry Trail

Quarry

Mesa Trail

Nature Trail, go right (north) onto the nature trail, dropping down some steps, then following the trail along the east side of Bluebell Canyon.

When you reach the Enchanted Mesa Trail at the stone bridge you passed at the outset of the hike, hitch right (east) about 20 feet to pick up the McClintock path, which plunges into the berries and willows that thrive along Bluebell Canyon's stream. A little footbridge crosses the creek and leads back to the trailhead at the auditorium.

## Miles and Directions

**0.0** Start by passing the gate and heading up the wide Enchanted Mesa Trail.

**0.2** Cross the bridge to the junction of the Enchanted Mesa and McClintock Nature Trails. Stay straight and uphill on the signed, obvious Enchanted Mesa service road.

**0.5** Pass the Enchanted Mesa welcome sign.

**1.0** The Kohler Mesa Trail crosses the Enchanted Mesa Trail. Stay straight (uphill) on the Enchanted Mesa Trail.

**1.2** Reach the signed junction of the Enchanted Mesa and Mesa Trails (also the Woods Quarry Trail). Go right on the Mesa Trail, passing an unsigned trail junction as you head down through the woods.

**1.4** At the junction with the McClintock Nature Trail, go right and downhill.

**1.7** At the unsigned Y, stay left and downhill on the McClintock Nature Trail.

**1.8** Reach the junction with the Enchanted Mesa Trail at the bridge. Go right (east) about 20 feet to pick up the lower portion of the nature trail, dropping into the riparian zone.

**2.0** At the first footbridge (at the boulder) go left, across the creek, then uphill.

**2.1** Arrive back at the trailhead.

# 8 Bluebell Mesa Loop

The focal point of this scenic and popular path is the beautiful meadow that sweeps down from the base of the First Flatiron. Springtime in the meadow brings forth a wildflower display that rivals any along the Front Range.

**Distance:** 1.5-mile loop
**Approximate hiking time:** 1 hour
**Difficulty:** Moderate due to a 520-foot elevation change
**Trail surface:** Paved roadway, dirt trail, and doubletrack
**Best seasons:** Spring through fall
**Other trail users:** None
**Canine compatibility:** Dogs permitted off-leash if displaying a Boulder Voice & Sight dog tag. Dogs must be leashed in the parking area.
**Fees and permits:** No fees or permits required
**Schedule:** Sunrise to sunset daily

**Trailhead facilities:** Paved parking lot, information signboard, visitor center with restrooms at the Ranger Cottage
**Maps:** USGS Eldorado Springs; Boulder Open Space and Mountain Parks Circle Hikes Guide
**Other:** The parking lot fills quickly on weekends. Additional parking is available along Baseline Road and on neighborhood streets.
**Trail contacts:** City of Boulder Open Space & Mountain Parks, P.O. Box 791, Boulder, CO 80306; (303) 441-3440; www.osmp.org

**Finding the trailhead:** From its intersection with Broadway (CO 93), go west on Baseline Road for 1.1 miles to the entrance to Chautauqua Park, which is on the left (south) side of the road. Parking and the trailhead are just inside the park entrance. GPS: N36 59.968' / W105 16.956'

# The Hike

Bluebell Mesa, with its quintessential Flatiron backdrop, is a classic Boulder hike. Iconic views and spectacular spring and summer wildflower displays conspire to satisfy nature lovers, trail runners, families, and couples looking for a little outdoor romance.

The loop can be hiked in either direction, but is described here clockwise, beginning on the paved Bluebell Canyon Road, a walk-and-talk "trail" that ascends south adjacent to Chautauqua Park's charming historic cottages. By the time you reach the Mesa Trail junction, the cottages have been left behind and stunning views of the Flatirons lie ahead.

The road forks at the Bluebell Shelter sign, making a loop up and around the shelter. A fragrant ponderosa parkland surrounds the shelter and the apex of the loop, including the Bluebell-Baird Trail, which you'll follow through the woods to the junction with the Bluebell Mesa Trail. The Bluebell Mesa Trail drops into the meadow.

The meandering descent through the meadow is the loop's highlight, with views stretching north along the Front Range and east across the Boulder Valley. The grasses bloom with a cycle of flowers, from lupine to bluebells to Indian paintbrush and mountain aster. Log stairs have been artfully set into the treadway, aiding in the descent and adding to the charm. Please do not pick the wildflowers—it is prohibited and also means the next hiker won't be able to enjoy them. The trail ends back at the parking area.

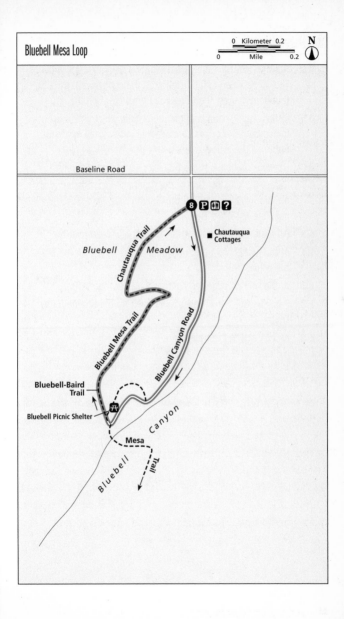

# Bluebell Mesa Loop

0 Kilometer 0.2
0 Mile 0.2

N

Baseline Road

8 P ♿ ?

Chautauqua Trail

Bluebell Meadow

Chautauqua Cottages

Bluebell Mesa Trail

Bluebell Canyon Road

Bluebell-Baird Trail

Bluebell Picnic Shelter

Canyon

Mesa

Bluebell Trail

# Miles and Directions

**0.0** Start by following the paved Bluebell Canyon Road uphill. The meadow and Flatirons are on the right (west); the Chautauqua cottages, then Bluebell Canyon, are on the left.

**0.5** Reach the junction with the Mesa Trail, which offers access to climbing routes and trails farther south. Stay right and uphill on the broad gravel path (also the Mesa Trail).

**0.6** Reach a trail split at the BLUEBELL SHELTER sign. Stay left.

**0.75** Reach the trail junction at the Bluebell Picnic Shelter, with an informational sign on the Flatirons. Go right on the wide, dirt Bluebell-Baird Trail.

**0.8** Go right and downhill on the signed Bluebell Mesa Trail.

**1.1** At the junction with an unsigned trail, stay left on the Bluebell Mesa Trail.

**1.2** At the trail junction, go right on the Chautauqua Trail.

**1.3** Pass the Ski Jump Trail, staying right on the Chautauqua Trail.

**1.5** Arrive back at the trailhead.

# 9 Gregory Canyon and Saddle Rock Loop

Awesome views and rugged terrain combine beautifully on one of the most challenging and rewarding day hikes in the Boulder area.

**Distance:** 3.7-mile loop
**Approximate hiking time:** 3 hours
**Difficulty:** More challenging
**Trail surface:** Dirt and rock trail
**Best seasons:** Late spring through fall
**Other trail users:** None
**Canine compatibility:** Dogs permitted off-leash on the trails if displaying a Boulder Voice & Sight dog tag. Dogs must be leashed in the parking area and on the E. M. Greenman Trail.
**Fees and permits:** Parking fee for vehicles not registered in Boulder County
**Schedule:** Sunrise to sunset daily
**Trailhead facilities:** Limited parking in the lot with additional parking along the access road,
restrooms, trash cans, picnic sites, information signboard
**Maps:** USGS Boulder and Eldorado Springs; Boulder Open Space & Mountain Parks Circle Hikes Guide; signboards at trail junctions
**Other:** Parking is limited and fills quickly on weekends. Additional parking is available along Baseline Road.
**Special considerations:** You will gain and lose more than 900 feet in elevation along the route. Don't attempt the loop if you have heart, respiratory, or knee problems.
**Trail contacts:** City of Boulder Open Space & Mountain Parks, P.O. Box 791, Boulder, CO 80306; (303) 441-3440; www .osmp.org

**Finding the trailhead:** From the intersection of Baseline Road and Broadway (CO 93), go west up Baseline Road for 1.3 miles, past the entrance to Chautauqua Park, to where the road turns sharply right and becomes Flagstaff Road at the base of Flagstaff Mountain. Turn left (southwest) onto the signed access road for Gregory Canyon. The trailhead is located at the end of the access road. GPS: N39 59.855' / W105 17.570'

## The Hike

Though not quite a mountaineering adventure, the challenging terrain of Gregory Canyon demands focus, and you'll work hard to earn views from the high points.

The trail is wild and steep from its outset, weaving west up the south-facing slope of the narrow canyon onto the forested slopes of Green Mountain. Setting a pace that suits your level of fitness is crucial to making this route easy, but no matter how slowly you go, the climb will generate sweat and muscle burn. Lest I have just put you off, remember that any mountain trail is only as hard as you make it. Drink plenty of water, rest and snack when you need to, and the trail is a piece of cake.

A very rewarding piece at that. The path, described here in a counterclockwise direction, is narrow and rocky but well kept, ascending amid wildflowers, poison ivy, and scattered shade from pines and firs. When you pause to rest (and you will), check out the views across the canyon to rock outcrops that jut out of the forest, or look east through the canyon mouth to the nearby metro area and the sprawling meadows of Chautauqua Park.

Keep an eye on your footing as you cross slabby sections and negotiate log-and-rock staircases that mitigate the trail's impressive elevation gain. A seasonal stream crossing at about the halfway point is a welcome respite, but the climb does not relent significantly for more than a mile, where it tops out—oh, be joyful—at the signed junction with the Ranger Trail.

The middle section of the hike is relatively flat, heading south on the Ranger Trail, a dirt road, to the old Green Mountain Lodge, where you will find restrooms, picnic tables, and a trail sign. Continue past the quaint and rustic lodge on the Ranger Trail, now a singletrack.

The Ranger Trail arcs southeast into tall evergreens, climbing a flight of log steps to its intersection with the E. M. Greenman Trail. Turn left onto the Greenman Trail. The trail traverses the forested east face of Green Mountain, then winds through a gully full of ferns and wild berries watered by a small stream. Many sensitive plant species grow along this portion of the route, so please stay on the trail and keep your dog on a leash.

Another set of rustic stairs leads to the intersection of Saddle Rock and Greenman Trails. Go left on the Saddle Rock Trail. The descent along the rocky dirt track features spectacular views down the canyon and onto the high plains, where the city of Boulder spreads across the flatlands like a quilt of silver and gray. This trail is also steep, so watch your footing and take your time.

Thick woodlands crowd out the views toward the end of the hike, and the final leg is through quiet forest. The Saddle Rock and Amphitheater Trails intersect not far above the trailhead. You can follow either trail to the base, but to check out rock climbers, go right (northeast) on the Amphitheater Trail. Otherwise, stay on the Saddle Rock Trail, which ends on the Gregory Canyon Trail in the riparian shade alongside the creek.

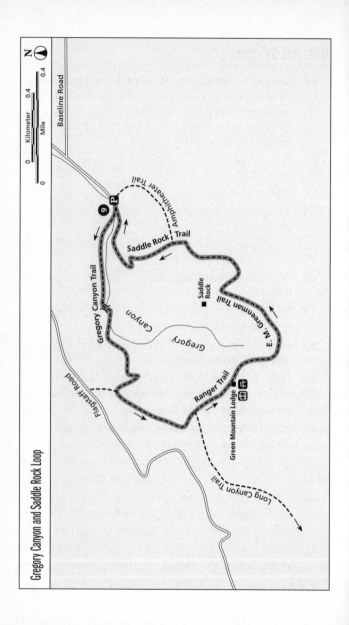

Gregory Canyon and Saddle Rock Loop

# Miles and Directions

**0.0**  Start on the Gregory Canyon Trail, heading west (to the right) out of the parking lot. The Amphitheater Trail also starts here, heading south (left). The trail splits within 100 feet; go right again on the Gregory Canyon Trail. (The left branch is the Saddle Rock Trail, the return route.)

**0.2**  At the junction with the Crown Rock Trail, stay left on the Gregory Canyon Trail.

**0.5**  Cross the stream via a bridge.

**1.1**  The trail flattens at the top of Gregory Canyon; cross the stream again.

**1.3**  At the signed junction with the Long Canyon and Ranger Trails, go left on the Ranger Trail.

**1.4**  Arrive at the Green Mountain Lodge. Stay left on the signed Ranger Trail.

**1.7**  Reach the E. M. Greenman Trail intersection. Go left on the Greenman trail toward Saddle Rock.

**2.3**  Arrive at the Saddle Rock Trail junction. Go left on Saddle Rock and begin the steep descent.

**3.0**  Reach the junction of the Amphitheater and Saddle Rock Trails. You can use either trail to reach the trailhead, but stay left to remain on the Saddle Rock Trail.

**3.7**  At the junction with the Gregory Canyon Trail, turn right. Another 100 feet and you're back at the trailhead.

# 10 Ute and Range View Trails (Flagstaff Mountain)

This easy, partially wheelchair–accessible, well–maintained path circumnavigates the summit of landmark Flagstaff Mountain and showcases Boulder's urban and wild sides.

**Distance:** 1.2-mile loop
**Approximate hiking time:** 45 minutes
**Difficulty:** Moderate due to some steep pitches on the Range View Trail
**Trail surface:** Wheelchair-accessible gravel path, dirt trail
**Best seasons:** Late spring, summer, fall
**Other trail users:** Wheelchair users
**Canine compatibility:** Dogs permitted off-leash if displaying a Boulder Voice & Sight dog tag. Dogs must be leashed in the parking area.
**Fees and permits:** Parking fee for cars not registered in Boulder County

**Schedule:** Sunrise to sunset daily
**Trailhead facilities:** Parking area, bike rack, fee station, information kiosk, dog waste station, picnic sites
**Maps:** USGS Boulder and Eldorado Springs; Boulder Open Space & Mountain Parks Circle Hikes Guide
**Special considerations:** Flagstaff Road is steep and winding and a favorite with cyclists. Be careful and courteous.
**Trail contacts:** City of Boulder Open Space & Mountain Parks, P.O. Box 791, Boulder, CO 80306; (303) 441-3440; www .osmp.org

**Finding the trailhead:** From the intersection of Baseline Road and Broadway (CO 93), drive west on Baseline for 1.3 miles, past the entrance to Chautauqua Park, to where it becomes Flagstaff Road at the foot of Flagstaff Mountain. Follow busy, scenic Flagstaff Road for about 3.5 miles to Realization Point. Parking areas are located on both sides of the road and fill quickly on summer weekends. The gated road to the summit of Flagstaff Mountain begins here as well, with additional parking and access to the trail loop at road's end. GPS (Flagstaff Road parking area): N39 59.844' / W105 18.546'

## The Hike

Looking east from Flagstaff Mountain, the high plains spread to the horizon, painted with the sprawling handiwork of humankind. Looking to the west, vistas of the snowy Indian Peaks and the steep, forested slopes of Boulder Canyon reach for the blue Colorado sky. The juxtaposition is thought provoking, and this trail is the perfect venue for its contemplation.

If you aren't inclined to be philosophical, you'll also find the loop is ideal for a family hike. It's short, with just enough rocky terrain to keep hikers focused; the views are spectacular; and the flora, fauna, and geology of the area are engaging, from fragrant ponderosa pine and prickly cactus to artful rock outcrops. Interpretive signs are posted on a portion of the route, and a significant section of the Ute Trail has been upgraded to make it wheelchair accessible.

The loop begins on the signed Ute Trail, located just uphill from the information kiosk and fee station. Climb through patches of meadow amid the ponderosas, with glimpses of the plains and the back side of the Flatirons visible through the trees. The trail loops past the junction with a side trail to an overlook before continuing toward the summit parking area (it is wheelchair accessible from this point on). The Ute Trail meets the Range View Trail at a five-way junction within sight of the summit parking and picnic areas.

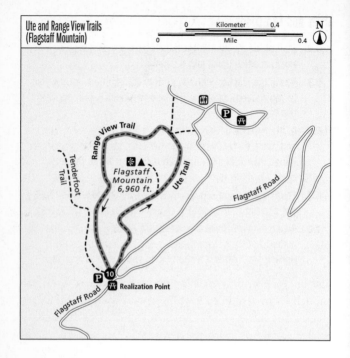

**Ute and Range View Trails**
**(Flagstaff Mountain)**

0             Kilometer      0.4

0              Mile          0.4

N

Range View Trail

Tenderfoot Trail

Flagstaff
Mountain
6,960 ft.

Ute Trail

Flagstaff Road

Flagstaff Road

10

Realization Point

Flagstaff Road

Range View Trail takes you back west, traversing the forested north and west faces of Flagstaff Mountain and passing several interpretive signs. Breaks in the woods offer stunning views of the Indian Peaks. This portion of the loop includes a rather steep, stair-step descent, with switchbacks posing more opportunities to enjoy the western panorama. Big boulders, part of a slow rockslide, dot the forest on the final stretch, which leads back to the picnic area and parking lot at the trailhead.

# Miles and Directions

**0.0** Start at the signed Ute trailhead above the information kiosk, heading uphill into the pines.

**0.3** Reach the junction with the path to the overlook. After a visit (if you choose), continue on the now-wheelchair-accessible Ute Trail.

**0.5** At the five-way junction with the Ute and Range View Trails and paths to the Flagstaff summit area, go left on the signed Range View Trail, past an interpretive sign about the tuft-eared Abert's squirrel.

**0.7** Pass an awesome vista point looking out onto Boulder Canyon and the snowcapped peaks of the Continental Divide.

**1.2** Reach the end of the descent at the junction with the Tenderfoot Trail in the picnic area below the Realization Point parking area. Go left; a short climb lands you back at the trailhead.

# 11 Meyers Homestead Trail (Walker Ranch)

Broad, green meadows, thick aspen glens, and the clear waters of a mountain stream shelter this gently ascending route to a viewpoint overlooking the snowcapped peaks of the Continental Divide.

**Distance:** 5.2 miles out and back

**Approximate hiking time:** 3 hours

**Difficulty:** Moderate due to trail length and a 740-foot elevation gain

**Trail surface:** Dirt ranch road

**Best seasons:** Late spring, summer, fall

**Other trail users:** Mountain bikers, equestrians

**Canine compatibility:** Leashed dogs permitted

**Fees and permits:** No fees or permits required

**Schedule:** Sunrise to sunset daily

**Trailhead facilities:** Large parking area, picnic tables and shelters, restrooms, trash cans, information kiosk with brochures

**Maps:** USGS Eldorado Springs; Walker Ranch brochure available at the trailhead

**Other:** The park offers tours of the Walker Ranch homestead and special events, including re-creations of ranch life in the late nineteenth century. Call (303) 776-8848 for more information.

**Trail contacts:** Boulder County Parks & Open Space, 5201 St. Vrain Rd., Longmont, CO 80503; (303) 678-6200; www.boulder countyopenspace.org

**Finding the trailhead:** From the intersection of Baseline Road and Broadway (CO 93), drive west on Baseline Road for 1.3 miles, past the entrance to Chautauqua Park, to where it becomes Flagstaff Road at the base of Flagstaff Mountain. Follow Flagstaff Road for about 7 miles to the signed Meyers Gulch trailhead, on the right (west) side of the road. Follow the dirt park road down to the lower parking area. GPS: N39 57.469' / W105 20.327'

## The Hike

To have homesteaded in this rugged high-country valley would have taken more energy and dedication than most hikers traveling the Meyers Homestead Trail today could ever muster. But the inspirational scenery, including classic Rocky Mountain views at trail's end, evoke the same passion for the wilderness those hardy pioneers must have felt.

Hikers, equestrians, and mountain bikers easily share this wide, gently ascending trail—a former ranch road. A scattering of interpretive signs dots the first section of trail, including one that describes the picturesque old sawmill cradled in a grassy basin. Timber harvested from the ranch was used in the mines, railroad spurs, and buildings of Colorado's gold rush.

The sawmill is the only former ranch building you'll see along the route. The homestead claim was made by James Walker in 1882 and was the seed of what became one of the largest cattle ranching operations in the area. Now on the National Register of Historic Places, the heart of the ranch, including the ranch house, barn, granary, and other outbuildings, is located at the Walker Ranch trailhead farther down Flagstaff Road. The ranch buildings are closed to the public but open for tours and special events.

A long, gentle climb begins just beyond the sawmill, following the stream and gulch up through evergreen woodlands and scattered aspen glens. It's a rolling, straightforward route, perfect for walking and talking. Near trail's end you'll climb through a gorgeous meadow. At the head of the

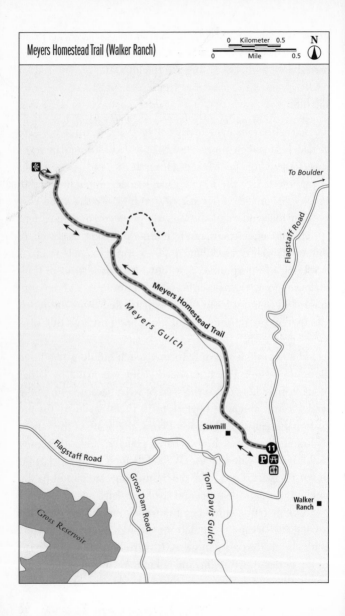

Meyers Homestead Trail (Walker Ranch)

0 Kilometer 0.5

0 Mile 0.5

N

To Boulder

Flagstaff Road

Meyers Homestead Trail

Meyers Gulch

Sawmill

11

P

Flagstaff Road

Gross Dam Road

Tom Davis Gulch

Walker Ranch

Gross Reservoir

meadow, the trail curves west and ends at a bench nestled among rocks and trees on the crest of a ridge. You can see past the bare cone of Sugarloaf Mountain to the Indian Peaks and north to the airy slopes of Longs Peak.

After you contemplate the scenery, follow the same trail back to the trailhead. The land beyond trail's end is private; please do not trespass.

## Miles and Directions

**0.0**  Start by heading down the ranch road into the meadow.

**0.5**  Pass the old sawmill.

**1.3**  Where a fire road breaks right, stay straight (left) on the Meyers Homestead Trail.

**1.9**  At the junction with a second fire road, stay left on the signed Meyers Homestead Trail.

**2.6**  Reach the overlook. Enjoy the views from the bench before retracing your steps.

**5.2**  Arrive back at the trailhead.

### Options

The 7.6-mile Walker Ranch Loop Trail offers a more challenging day hike for those up to the task. The trail intersects the Eldorado Canyon Trail, which drops into Eldorado Canyon State Park. Check out the Walker Ranch brochure for more information.

# 12  Boulder Creek Greenway Path

The Boulder Creek Greenway Path is Boulder's busiest, most colorful recreational passageway. This short hike begins at the mouth of Boulder Canyon and ends downtown, looping back via a short jaunt along the Pearl Street Mall.

**Distance:** 2.6-mile lollipop
**Approximate hiking time:** 1.5 hours
**Difficulty:** Easy
**Trail surface:** Wheelchair-accessible concrete pavement; gravel trail
**Best seasons:** Year-round
**Other trail users:** Cyclists, in-line skaters, runners
**Canine compatibility:** Leashed dogs permitted
**Fees and permits:** No fees or permits required
**Schedule:** All day, every day
**Trailhead facilities:** Paved parking area, restrooms, trash cans, picnic sites, information signboards, playing greens, tot lot, beach
**Maps:** USGS Boulder; Boulder Open Space & Mountain Parks Trail Map, available online at www.osmp.org
**Other:** The trail is wheelchair accessible. It's also usually very crowded; please observe proper trail etiquette and be courteous to other trail users. The trailhead parking lot fills quickly on weekends; additional parking is available along nearby side streets.
**Trail contacts:** City of Boulder Open Space & Mountain Parks, P.O. Box 791, Boulder, CO 80306; (303) 441-3440; www.osmp.org

**Finding the trailhead:** From the junction of US 36 and Canyon Boulevard (CO 119) in downtown Boulder, head west on Canyon Boulevard for about 1 mile to Pearl Street. Go right on Pearl Street and then left into the signed parking area for Settler's Park. A trail leads west from Settler's Park, under Canyon Boulevard, to the greenway trail on the south side of Boulder Creek at the west end of Eben G. Fine Park. GPS (for Settler's Park): N40 00.836' / W105 17.721'. GPS (for the path in Eben G. Fine Park): N40 00.768' / W105 17.734'

## The Hike

If people on foot were considered Boulder's lifeblood, the Boulder Creek Greenway Path would be a major artery. Tracing the course of Boulder Creek from Boulder Canyon through downtown and out into the eastern residential areas, the scenic paved trail pulses day and night with activity and local color.

Human-powered conveyances of all designs (wheelchairs, strollers, skates, and a variety of bicycles) roll along the path, which is impossible to get lost on. Trail runners test their legs and lungs on the trail, and college students use it to get to and from the university. On hot summer days families and friends launch tubes and inflatable rafts into the creek. Residents and tourists alike stroll through the shade of cottonwood and willow, sharing stories and detouring into downtown for coffee or a bite to eat.

This tour of the path begins in Settler's Park, at the mouth of Boulder Canyon. Follow the trail link from Settler's Park, under Canyon Boulevard and into Eben G. Fine Park, where you meet the greenway trail and turn left toward downtown Boulder. Shady lawns sweep down to the creek in Fine community park, where rafters and tubers begin leisurely floats downstream.

Cross a bridge spanning the creek at the eastern edge of Fine park, then pick up the gravel path restricted to foot traffic (parallel to the paved trail), and head downstream through the riparian zone. Benches offer opportunities to watch the sun flicker on the riffles in the creek. A diversion

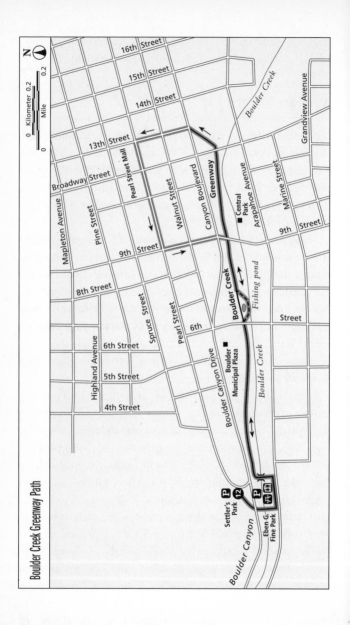

Boulder Creek Greenway Path

dam allows the creek to pool into a fishing lagoon, which has been artfully surrounded by benches, lawns, and fishing platforms. As you approach Ninth Street you'll encounter the Charles A. Haertling Sculpture Park.

As green and lovely as this walk is, it can't be mistaken for a wilderness trek. The borders of the greenbelt are distinctly urban, with Boulder's Municipal Plaza, shops and offices, and busy Canyon Boulevard (CO 119) on the north side. Rather than avoiding the cityscape, this loop embraces it, diverging onto the enlivening Pearl Street Mall for a stretch.

The pedestrian-only mall is lined with charming shops and restaurants. On weekends, holidays, and sometimes during the week, street performers—jugglers, contortionists, musicians, magicians, and the like—entertain passersby. Follow Pearl Street past Broadway back to 9th Street, then hook left along 9th to the bike path, which leads back to the trailhead.

## Miles and Directions

**0.0** Start in Settler's Park. From the parking lot go west along the concrete trail and use the pedestrian tunnel to cross under Canyon Boulevard and enter Eben G. Fine Park.

**0.2** Turn left onto the paved greenway trail in Eben G. Fine Park, heading east. Cross a bridge spanning Boulder Creek, passing an informational sign.

**0.3** Go right onto the gravel hikers-only path, where there is another bridge crossing. The wheelchair-accessible route sticks to the pavement.

**0.6** Pass the Boulder County government offices and Justice Center.

**0.7** Go right, over the bridge at the diversion dam, onto a little island in the stream. The creek flows on the right; the fishing pond is on the left.

**0.8** Swing left over the bridge that spans the lagoon's outlet, and then go right to continue on the gravel path. Drop under the 9th Street bridge.

**1.1** The dirt track ends at the Broadway bridge. Pick up the paved trail, staying right, and drop through the cool creek-side underpass to cross under Broadway.

**1.2** Pass the Central Park band shell and lawns. At 13th Street go left, following the sidewalk and crosswalks across Canyon Boulevard and Walnut Street to the pedestrian Pearl Street Mall.

**1.3** Go left on the mall, window-shopping and people watching as you proceed westward. The pedestrian-only section ends at 11th Street; continue west using the Pearl Street side-walk.

**1.7** At 9th Street go left for 3 blocks. Cross Canyon Boulevard and close the loop at the bridge, picking up the paved greenway path by dropping down under the bridge. From here, retrace your steps.

**2.6** Arrive back at the trailhead.

## Options

The path continues west into Boulder Canyon, offering more of a workout as it climbs into more mountainous terrain. Farther east, the trail links neighborhoods to schools, shopping areas, and parklands.

# 13 Sanitas Valley and Dakota Ridge Trails

Find relative seclusion just minutes from downtown Boulder on this easy hike in the Sanitas Valley, with the Dakota Hogback forming a natural barrier between the parkland and an adjacent historic neighborhood.

**Distance:** 2.3-mile lollipop
**Approximate hiking time:** 1.5 hours
**Difficulty:** Easy
**Trail surface:** Dirt road and trail
**Best seasons:** Spring through fall
**Other trail users:** Trail runners
**Canine compatibility:** Dogs permitted off-leash on trails if displaying a Boulder Voice & Sight dog tag. Dogs must be leashed in trailhead areas.
**Fees and permits:** No fees or permits required
**Schedule:** Sunrise to sunset daily. The Centennial parking area is closed from midnight to 5 a.m.

**Trailhead facilities:** Parking is available along the road near the information signboard just beyond Boulder Community Hospital and 0.2 mile farther up Mapleton at the Centennial trailhead, which also has restrooms, picnic facilities, and information signboards.
**Maps:** USGS Boulder; Boulder Open Space & Mountain Parks Circle Hikes Guide
**Trail contacts:** City of Boulder Open Space & Mountain Parks, P.O. Box 791, Boulder, CO 80306; (303) 441-3440; www .osmp.org

**Finding the trailhead:** From the intersection of Baseline Road and Broadway (CO 93), follow Broadway north for 1.8 miles to Mapleton Avenue. Go left (west) on Mapleton Avenue for 0.8 mile, passing Boulder Community Hospital, to parking alongside the road. The trailhead is a few yards west of the hospital. GPS (parking near Boulder Community Hospital): N40 01.241' / W105 17.633'

## The Hike

The Dakota Hogback, the first significant rise of the Rocky Mountains, is a fixture of the mountain backdrop along the Front Range. In Boulder the hogback is overshadowed by the Flatirons, but the rolling ridge gains prominence as you move north, beginning here in Sanitas Valley at the mouth of Sunshine Canyon.

The hogback ridge forms the east wall of little Sanitas Valley, with Mount Sanitas forming the western border. The valley is narrow and sloping, watered by a seasonal stream and ditch, and site of wildflower blooms in spring and summer. The wide trail is perfect for walking and talking, with rest benches set along the way.

Near the head of the valley, where homes have been built on a neighboring ridge with views down Sanitas Valley, the Dakota Ridge Trail breaks off to the right. Several overlooks, one with a bench, afford views of Boulder and the high plains to the east and Mount Sanitas to the west.

Following the Dakota Ridge Trail back downvalley, views open through the sparse pines to the Flatirons. The setting is quite different from that on the adjacent valley floor, shaded by the evergreens and traversing below rock faces where climbers practice their acrobatic skills. Several paths break right to the parallel Sanitas Valley Trail.

The valley trail is very popular with dogs and their walkers. Dogs are able to run off-leash if under strict voice and sight control, and the ditch offers cool water for drinking or a belly dip (but only for canines). With trail runners, rock climbers, and mountain bikers (prohibited, but the trail is

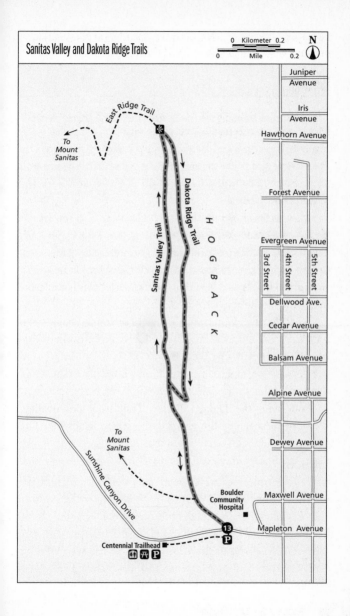

poached) also on the route, be prepared to share the trail and observe proper etiquette.

## Miles and Directions

**0.0** Start by following the short access trail to the broad Sanitas Valley Trail at the information signboard.

**0.1** Pass the first junction with the signed Mount Sanitas Trail. Stay right on the Sanitas Valley Trail. A second junction with the trail to the peak follows shortly. Again stay right.

**0.2** Cross the ditch.

**0.3** Pass the first junction with the Dakota Ridge Trail. Stay left on the broad Sanitas Valley Trail.

**0.6** Pass another Dakota Ridge Trail spur, again staying left.

**1.1** Reach the junction of the Sanitas Valley, Dakota Ridge Trail, and East Ridge Trail (which leads to the summit of Mount Sanitas), near the top of the valley. Go right on the Dakota Ridge Trail.

**1.6** Pass the first trail link down to the Sanitas Valley Trail. Stay left on the rocky, traversing Dakota Ridge Trail.

**1.8** Pass another junction with a link to the Sanitas Valley Trail.

**2.1** Follow switchbacks down to the lowest junction with the Sanitas Valley Trail. Go left on the Sanitas Valley Trail, retracing your steps to the trailhead.

**2.3** Arrive back at the trailhead.

### Options

If you want more of a challenge (and workout), include the Mount Sanitas Trail in your loop. Steep and rocky both on the ascent and the descent, the trail involves about 1,200 feet in elevation gain and sports great views of the high plains to the east and the Indian Peaks to the west. A loop including the Mount Sanitas and Sanitas Valley Trails totals 3.1 miles.

# 14 Sugarloaf Mountain

Views from the windswept summit of this foothills peak sweep west to encompass the arc of the Continental Divide and east onto the high plains.

**Distance:** 1.4 miles out and back

**Approximate hiking time:** 1 hour

**Difficulty:** Moderate due to a 500-foot elevation change

**Trail surface:** Rocky dirt road

**Best seasons:** Summer and fall

**Other trail users:** Mountain bikers, equestrians

**Canine compatibility:** Leashed dogs permitted

**Fees and permits:** No fees or permits required

**Schedule:** Sunrise to sunset daily

**Trailhead facilities:** Dirt parking area

**Maps:** USGS Gold Hill

**Trail contacts:** Arapahoe and Roosevelt National Forest, Boulder Ranger District, 2140 Yarmouth Ave., Boulder, CO 80301; (303) 541-2500; fs.usda.gov

Boulder County Parks & Open Space, 5201 St. Vrain Rd., Longmont, CO 80503; (303) 678-6200; www.bouldercounty openspace.org

**Finding the trailhead:** From the intersection of Broadway and Canyon Boulevard (CO 119) in downtown Boulder, go left (west) on CO 119 into Boulder Canyon. Drive 5 miles up the canyon to Sugarloaf Road. Go right on Sugarloaf Road for 4.8 miles to Sugarloaf Mountain Road. Go right (east) on Sugarloaf Mountain Road for 0.8 mile to the small unsigned parking area for the Sugarloaf Mountain and Switzerland trailheads. GPS: N40 01.518' / W105 25.520'

## The Hike

The top of Sugarloaf Mountain is exhilaratingly exposed—a jumbled hump of talus that drops away precipitously on all

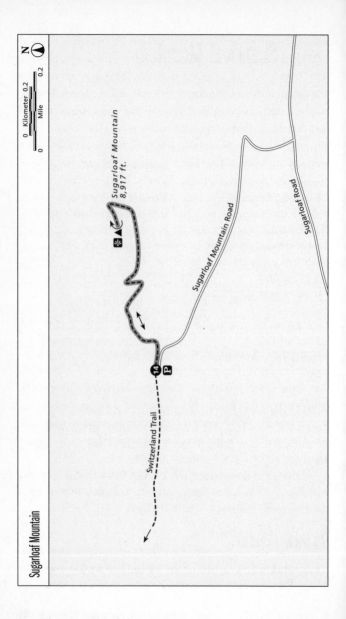

Sugarloaf Mountain

sides. The views will leave you awestruck. The jagged summits of the Indian Peaks rise to the west, and the high plains flow east from the wooded foothills. The devastation of a late-twentieth-century forest fire has faded, but a burled, charred tree trunk still clings to the mountainside, and the slopes and surroundings remain relatively naked. New growth, including pioneering stands of aspen, has taken root amid the few remaining silvered snags. The area charred in 2010's Fourmile Fire can also be surveyed from the summit.

The route is straightforward, following a rugged mining road that curves up and eastward from the parking area. Don't worry about the forks at the outset—all paths merge by the time the road rounds the first switchback. The steady switchbacking climb leads through sparse woodland carpeted with kinnikinnick and small, low-growing wildflowers. Views to the west are of the Continental Divide.

At about 0.3 mile the trees end and the road begins a traverse across the old burn zone. Talus spreads uphill and down from the path. Circle onto the east face, still climbing; views open of the high plains. At the next switchback the flatland vistas give way to a snowcapped panorama. And when you reach the rocky summit you can survey 360 degrees of Rocky Mountain splendor. A cluster of wind-sculpted evergreens hunkers on the west edge of the peak, a prime shelter for savoring the views.

Descend via the same route. It's all downhill, but the rocky footing is demanding. Your eyes will be drawn from the trail to the views, but try to concentrate . . .

## Miles and Directions

**0.0** Start by walking uphill on the fire road labeled 800, passing the chain that blocks access to motorized vehicles. Pass another gated access about 300 feet uphill. The trail splits and rejoins.

**0.3** Views open down into Boulder Canyon and up into the Indian Peaks. Ignore side trails and keep climbing, negotiating two switchbacks on the west face.

**0.4** Pass a Boulder County parks sign.

**0.5** Pass a bench.

**0.7** Arrive on the summit. Take in the views and then return as you came.

**1.4** Arrive back at the trailhead.

## Options

The Switzerland Trail shares the Sugarloaf trailhead. The trail—an old narrow-gauge railroad line linking Sugarloaf Mountain with points north and west, including Gold Hill—is a popular hiking and mountain biking route.

Nearby Betasso Preserve, also located off Sugarloaf Road, offers a nice short hike on the 3.2-mile, multiuse Canyon Loop Trail.

# 15 Pines to Peaks Trail (Bald Mountain Scenic Area)

Views from the summit meadow of this short loop are among the best in Boulder's backyard, ranging west to the Indian Peaks; south to the back side of Flagstaff Mountain and the Flatirons; and east to Boulder, Denver, and surrounding plains. With about half the preserve burned in the 2010 Fourmile Fire, the trail will offer instruction on fire ecology in the years to come.

**Distance:** 1.1-mile lollipop
**Approximate hiking time:** 45 minutes
**Difficulty:** Easy
**Trail surface:** Dirt singletrack
**Best seasons:** Late spring, summer, and fall
**Other trail users:** None
**Canine compatibility:** Leashed dogs permitted
**Fees and permits:** No fees or permits required
**Schedule:** Sunrise to sunset daily

**Trailhead facilities:** Dirt parking lot, portable restroom, picnic sites, information signboard
**Maps:** USGS Boulder; trail map available online at www.bouldercounty.org/openspace/recreating/public_parks/parks_pdfs/web_baldmtn.pdf
**Trail contacts:** Boulder County Parks and Open Space, 5201 St. Vrain Rd., Longmont, CO 80503; (303) 678-6200; www.bouldercounty.org/openspace

**Finding the trailhead:** From the intersection of Broadway and Baseline Road, follow Broadway (CO 93) north for 1.8 miles to Mapleton Avenue. Go left (west) on Mapleton Avenue into Sunshine Canyon; Mapleton becomes Sunshine Canyon Drive at the canyon mouth. Follow Mapleton/Sunshine Canyon Drive for a total of 4.7

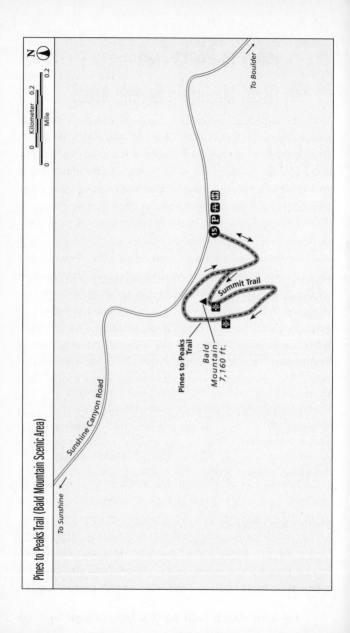

Pines to Peaks Trail (Bald Mountain Scenic Area)

To Sunshine

Sunshine Canyon Road

Pines to Peaks Trail

Bald
Mountain
7,160 ft.

Summit Trail

To Boulder

N

0        Kilometer        0.2

0        Mile        0.2

miles to the signed parking lot for the Bald Mountain Scenic Area on the left (south) side of the road. GPS: N40 02.859' / W105 20.476'

# The Hike

Prior to 2010's Fourmile Fire, Bald Mountain was reminiscent of a textbook case of male pattern baldness. A ponderosa forest circled its base like a fringe of hair around a shiny pate. In the wake of the most destructive wildfire in Colorado's history, about fifty percent of the terrain was burned. Now it's a textbook case in fire ecology.

Wind, seasonal weather extremes, coarse, shallow soil, and most recently the Fourmile Fire have conspired to keep the summit of Bald Mountain a tree-free zone. This relative lack of cover has its advantages: The views are superlative in all directions, and wildflowers bloom prolifically in season. A thoughtfully placed bench in a stand of ponderosa pines—which amazingly survived the 2010 conflagration—is a perfect viewpoint, facing the high plains and overlooking Denver, which glitters like the Emerald City in the distance. The east side of the preserve was relatively untouched by the fire.

The loop is straightforward, beginning in the woodland at the base of the peak. The trail forks within 0.1 mile, with the signed Summit Trail climbing to the bench and viewpoint.

The route then drops through meadow and circles onto the back (west) side of the mountain, where fire consumed trees, shrubs, and meadow. On the upside, wonderful views of the saw-toothed peaks of the Continental Divide rise above the fire zone. A final traverse along the north face of the mountain, looking down on canyons and foothills properties ravaged by the Fourmile blaze, leads back to the trailhead. Vegetation on these slopes will slowly regenerate, beginning with annual wildflowers and meadow grasses, progressing through hardy shrubs and aspen glens, and, if man and nature permit, culminating in a climax woodland.

## Miles and Directions

**0.0** Start by climbing steps to the information signboard at the trailhead, then going left (south) around the picnic area on the singletrack. A second path through the picnic area joins the Pines to Peaks Trail within the first 0.1 mile.

**0.1** At the Y go left and uphill on the Summit Trail. You will return on the Pines to Peaks Trail, which heads right.

**0.3** Arrive on the summit at the memory bench. Take in the views and then follow the obvious singletrack downhill to the south. Ignore the side trail that breaks left to the fenced property line, staying right and circling onto the west face of the peak.

**0.7** Views open west to the snowy divide.

**1.0** Close the loop at the junction with the Summit Trail, having circled the north and east faces of the peak. Turn left to return to the trailhead.

**1.1** Arrive back at the trailhead.

# 16 Walden Ponds Wildlife Habitat

A nice trail system, including an interpretive boardwalk, rambles through a wildlife habitat built around ponds that were once gravel pits.

**Distance:** 1.4-mile lollipop
**Approximate hiking time:** 1 hour
**Difficulty:** Easy
**Trail surface:** Overgrown double-track, gravel road, boardwalk
**Best seasons:** Year-round
**Other trail users:** Equestrians, mountain bikers, anglers
**Canine compatibility:** Leashed dogs permitted
**Fees and permits:** No fees or permits required
**Schedule:** Sunrise to sunset daily
**Trailhead facilities:** Parking lot, restrooms, trash cans, picnic sites, dog waste station, information sign
**Maps:** USGS Niwot; map in the brochure available at the trailhead and online at www .bouldercounty.org/openspace/ recreating/public_parks/parks_ pdfs/WaldenPonds.pdf
**Other:** Catch-and-release fishing is permitted in all ponds. Wally Toevs Pond is restricted to use by senior citizens and handi-capped individuals. Swimming is prohibited. The field station at the center of the preserve is closed to the public.
**Trail contacts:** Boulder County Parks and Open Space, 5201 St. Vrain Rd., Longmont, CO 80503; 303-678-6200; www.boulder county.org/openspace

**Finding the trailhead:** From US 36 in north Boulder, go right (east) on Jay Road. Follow Jay Road for 4.3 miles to 75th Street. Turn right onto 75th Street and go 0.5 mile to the signed Walden Ponds Wildlife Habitat on the right. GPS: N40 02.642' / W105 11.027'

# The Hike

In a world where it often seems that nature is losing out to development, the Walden Ponds Wildlife Habitat and neighboring Sawhill Ponds are a refreshing confirmation that sometimes the opposite is the case.

The ponds are not only in a distinctly urban setting but also were born of "progress." Their evolution was relatively swift. In the early 1950s (and for decades before), the acreage along the Boulder Creek drainage was pastureland and hayfields. By the 1960s, as population boomed along the Front Range, the area was mined extensively for gravel used in road building. When the gravel was depleted in the 1970s, the area began its journey back to a more natural state.

The Walden Ponds reclamation project was initiated by Boulder County in 1974, and over the years six ponds, with islands and marshlands, were sculpted from the remaining mined rock. Rain and meltwater filled the depressions, trees and shrubs were planted . . . and before long, a wildlife habitat capable of supporting a variety of bird, fish, insect, and mammal species had taken shape where once there was only rubble.

Gravel operations continue on the periphery of the wildlife sanctuary, and beyond the fenced border of the preserve you'll see a number of other ponds/former gravel pits. Views of adjacent industry occasionally intrude, but the trails are mostly insulated by thick stands of cottonwood and willow. This lollipop hike begins at Cottonwood Marsh and encircles Pelican Marsh, Bass Pond, and Island Lake before returning to the trailhead. (The loop portion can be hiked in either direction but is described here clockwise.) The boardwalk winding through cattails on the open water in Cottonwood Marsh is lined with interpretive signs.

## Miles and Directions

**0.0** Start by heading east, past the information sign and covered picnic area, on the Cottonwood Marsh Trail. At the end of the boardwalk, go right onto a signed viewing platform.

**0.25** Leave the boardwalk and follow the short trail to the field station (closed to the public). This is the start of the loop. Go left on the broad track toward Pelican Marsh. (Duck Pond is on the left.) A fenceline and marker delineate the border between Sawhill and Walden Ponds. Stay on the right side of the fence, on an overgrown doubletrack headed west toward the mountain front.

**0.5** Reach Pelican Marsh and the signed Ricky Weiser Wetlands. At the junction with the trail into the Sawhill Ponds, go right (north), following the trail atop the levee bordering Pelican Marsh. Another pond, with a gravel island that hearkens back to the area's previous incarnation, lies over the fence-line to the west.

**0.8** The trail turns east to trace the pond's north shore.

**0.9** At the junction with a social trail, stay straight on the mowed doubletrack, passing Bass Pond on the right.

**1.0** Head sharply right (south) on the levee-top track, with Bass Pond on the right and Cottonwood Marsh on the left.

**1.25** Complete the loop at the trail junction at the field station. Go left to retrace your steps back to the boardwalk.

**1.4** Arrive back at the trailhead.

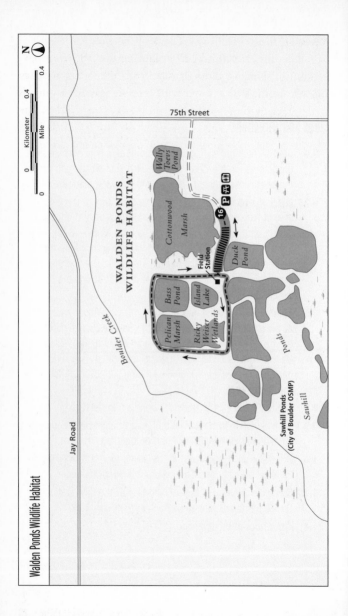

Walden Ponds Wildlife Habitat

## Options

You can extend your hike by venturing into the neighboring Sawhill Ponds preserve, a City of Boulder Open Space and Mountain Parks property. Access to Sawhill Ponds is at the field station junction near Duck Pond and at the southwest corner of the Walden Ponds preserve on Pelican Marsh. Adding a loop through Sawhill would add about 1.0 mile to the excursion.

# 17  Wonderland Lake

Easy, scenic, and friendly, the trail circling Wonderland Lake borders a wildlife sanctuary and skirts the base of the Dakota Hogback.

**Distance:** 1.75-mile lollipop
**Approximate hiking time:** 1 hour
**Difficulty:** Easy
**Trail surface:** Packed gravel, dirt trail, pavement, sidewalk
**Best seasons:** Year-round
**Other trail users:** Mountain bikers
**Canine compatibility:** Leashed dogs permitted
**Fees and permits:** No fees or permits required
**Schedule:** Sunrise to sunset daily
**Trailhead facilities:** Gravel parking lot, picnic sites, dog waste station, information signboard
**Maps:** USGS Boulder; trail map available online at www.osmp.org
**Other:** The trail is wheelchair accessible. Fishing is permitted from the dam and peninsula. Swimming in the lake is prohibited.
**Trail contacts:** City of Boulder Open Space & Mountain Parks, P.O. Box 791, Boulder, CO 80306; (303) 441-3440; www.osmp.org

**Finding the trailhead:** From the intersection of Broadway and Baseline Road, take Broadway (CO 93) north for about 3.5 miles to the Wonderland Lake trailhead (on the left/west side of Broadway north of Quince Avenue and south of Utica Street). The trailhead parking lot fronts the Foothills Nature Center building. GPS: N40 03.067' / W105 16.943'

## The Hike

Like a familiar neighborhood stroll, the trail around Wonderland Lake wraps you in ease and comfort. The perfect choice for a summer evening, when the foothills are backlit by the setting sun, the lake trail and adjacent paths are popular with trail runners and families.

Surrounded on three sides by suburban development, the area has enjoyed long success as a wildlife sanctuary, offering safe harbor to a variety of species from songbirds to rattlesnakes. Tread with care. Ecosystems include riparian habitat, wetland, and prairie, which bloom with colorful wildflowers in spring and summer. The circuit also includes a neighborhood park with manicured greens and a tot lot and a short stretch on a residential street. The easy melding of suburbia and wildland is thought-provoking and hopeful.

The well-signed lollipop route begins by following the gravel Foothills Nature Center Trail west toward the lake and the abrupt swell of the Dakota Hogback. The loop portion is described here in a clockwise direction, beginning with the short trail that winds out through the grasses and willows on the fishing peninsula. Back on the Wonderland Lake Trail, cross the earthen dam and watch for deer in the meadow below and to the east.

On the south side of the lake, the trail intersects concrete paths leading into adjacent neighborhoods. You'll find manicured lawns, a playground, and benches along this section of the route.

Leaving the pavement behind, the trail heads north on a gravel track along the lake's west shore, where a split-rail fence on one side guards the verdant, birdsong-filled wetland and the Dakota Hogback marks the first rise in the Front Range on the other. The trail junction at the northwest edge of the lake offers access to the popular Foothills Trail, which runs for several miles along the hogback in north Boulder.

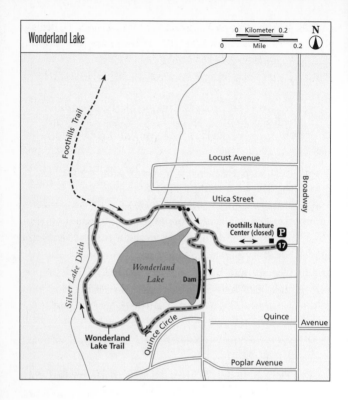

The final section of the loop branches onto a residential street before hooking back into the sanctuary near the start of the loop. Back at the Foothills Nature Center Trail, retrace your steps to the trailhead.

## Miles and Directions

**0.0** Start by following the Foothills Nature Center Trail west past the nature center toward Wonderland Lake.

**0.25** At the junction on the lakeshore, go left and down the steps. Walk about 50 feet to the next trail intersection and go right on the gravel spur that explores the peninsula.

**0.3** The peninsula path ends. Go right on the Wonderland Lake Trail, across the dam.

**0.5** Leave the sanctuary at the sign and continue on the paved trail. Stay right at all junctions with concrete paths leading into adjacent neighborhoods, circling the lake in a clockwise direction.

**0.7** Cross a little bridge over an inlet, then arrive at a trail junction. Go right, around the playground.

**0.9** Another right turn leads onto the signed, gravel Wonderland Lake Trail. An information signboard marks sanctuary boundary. The lake is on the right; on the left, the Silver Lake Ditch traverses the base of the hogback.

**1.1** Cross the ditch to the junction with the Foothills Trail. Go right, following the trail into the residential area.

**1.3** The trail parallels a private drive to the Utica Avenue sidewalk. Follow the sidewalk right (east).

**1.4** Go right onto the Wonderland Lake Trail at the sign, passing through a gate.

**1.5** Return to the trail junction at the dam and peninsula. Go left onto the gravel nature center trail.

**1.75** Arrive back at the trailhead.

# 18 Sage and Eagle Trail Loop (Boulder Valley Ranch)

The high prairie setting of this easy loop, which follows dirt roads through a working ranch, hearkens back to frontier days. Watch for songbirds and raptors around the stock pond and for thunderheads building over the foothills.

**Distance:** 2.8-mile loop
**Approximate hiking time:** 2 hours
**Difficulty:** Easy
**Trail surface:** Gravel ranch roads
**Best seasons:** Year-round, although snow or rain may make the route muddy
**Other trail users:** Mountain bikers, equestrians
**Canine compatibility:** Dogs permitted off-leash on trails if displaying a Boulder Voice & Sight dog tag. Dogs must be leashed in trailhead areas.

**Fees and permits:** No fees or permits required
**Schedule:** Sunrise to sunset daily
**Trailhead facilities:** Parking lot, restrooms, trash cans, information signboard
**Maps:** USGS Boulder; trail map available online at www.osmp.org
**Trail contacts:** City of Boulder Open Space & Mountain Parks, P.O. Box 791, Boulder, CO 80306; (303) 441-3440; www.osmp.org

**Finding the trailhead:** From the freeway interchange at Baseline Road and US 36, go north on US 36 for 6 miles. Turn right (east) onto Longhorn Road (at the sign for the park). Follow Longhorn Road, which begins as pavement and becomes a gravel road after 0.2 mile, for a total of 1 mile to the trailhead parking area, on the right (south) side of the road. GPS: N40 04.790' / W105 15.764'

# The Hike

When you think of Boulder, mountains spring to mind. But in fact, the city lies mostly on flatlands—flatlands that are arguably as beautiful as the highlands but in a very different way.

Boulder Valley Ranch epitomizes the beauty and solitude of the high plains. Though surrounded by signs of civilization, the park's trails are embraced by prairie. Grasses wave gold or green, depending on the season, and are thick with wildflowers in spring and early summer. Birds dip to drink or swim at the stock pond, and the rounded summits of the foothills line the western horizon.

With a bit of luck you will find yourself alone here. And with a bit of imagination, you can transport yourself back to a time when, rather than sprawling suburbia, this was all there was along Colorado's Front Range.

This route links the Sage and Eagle Trails in a relatively flat, easy loop. The path follows a well-maintained roadbed still used by the rancher who runs livestock on the property. In addition to domestic animals and prairie dogs, migratory waterfowl and other birds, including raptors, frequent the property.

The hike begins on the Sage Trail, which heads south. Tall grass and yucca line the west side of the road; blowsy cottonwoods drink from the Farmers Ditch that runs along the east side. Where the trees break you can see the open prairie stretching toward the Boulder Reservoir, east of the park.

Pass a gate and cross the ditch to pick up the Eagle Trail. Swing east and then north, passing through waist-high prairie grasses to the pond. Rest awhile on the pond's dam at

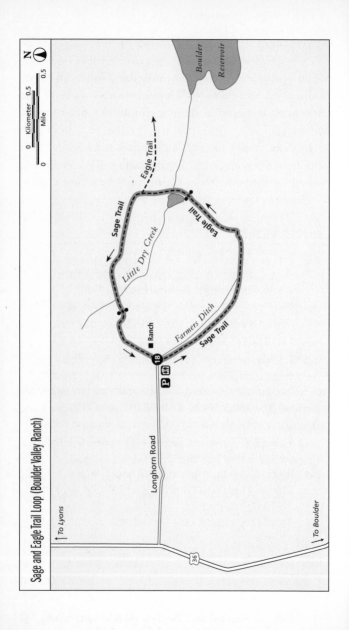

Sage and Eagle Trail Loop (Boulder Valley Ranch)

the bottom of the shallow, grassy bowl—for as long as the biting bugs allow. It's an inviting place to sit and contemplate a landscape reminiscent of the fabled American West.

Back on the Sage Trail, on high ground above the pond, walk west toward the ragged foothills, often topped with voluminous clouds that may or may not form into purple-bottomed thunderheads. When you reach the ranch buildings, stay right (north), passing through gated cattle enclosures on the north boundary of the ranch complex. The loop ends back at the parking area.

## Miles and Directions

**0.0** Start on the signed Sage Trail. Within a few yards you'll pass the junction with the Cobalt Trail, which departs to the right. The Sage Trail parallels the ditch, heading south.

**0.6** Reach the intersection with the Eagle Trail. Stay straight, crossing the ditch, now on the Eagle Trail heading east.

**0.9** Pass a gate into a prairie dog town.

**1.3** A long, easy meander drops to the pond's dam. Go through the gate, cross the dam, and then go up through a second gate. A social trail breaks left to the levee top; stay right and follow the formal trail up to the sign and another gate.

**1.6** On top of the levee at the junction of the Sage and Eagle Trails, go left on the Sage Trail. The right fork (Eagle Trail) leads toward the Boulder Reservoir.

**2.4** Back at the ranch, follow the signed Sage Trail through the gate and along the fenceline. You may share the trail with lowing, grazing bovines.

**2.8** Climb to the last gate, cross the road, and arrive back at the trailhead.

# 19  Lichen Loop (Heil Valley Ranch)

A perfect outing for families, this interpretive trail tours a mountain meadow in the shadow of the hogback north of the Boulder city limits.

**Distance:** 1.6-mile lollipop

**Approximate hiking time:** 1 hour

**Difficulty:** Easy

**Trail surface:** Dirt singletrack

**Best seasons:** Spring through fall

**Other trail users:** None.

**Canine compatibility:** Dogs not permitted

**Fees and permits:** No fees or permits required

**Schedule:** Sunrise to sunset daily

**Trailhead facilities:** Large loop parking lot, restrooms, picnic sites, trash cans, information signboards with maps

**Maps:** USGS Boulder; trail map available online at www.bouldercounty.org/openspace/recreating/public_parks/parks_pdfs/HeilKioskMap.pdf

**Other:** Other park routes are popular and heavily used by mountain bikers and equestrians.

**Trail contacts:** Boulder County Parks and Open Space, 5201 St. Vrain Rd., Longmont, CO 80503; (303) 678-6200; www.bouldercounty.org/openspace

**Finding the trailhead:** From the intersection of US 36 and Canyon Boulevard (CO 119) in downtown Boulder, head north on US 36 for 8.6 miles to Lefthand Canyon Road. Turn left (west) onto Lefthand Canyon Road and go 0.6 mile to a right turn onto Geer Canyon Road. Follow Geer Canyon Road for 1.1 miles (the first 0.2 are paved; the rest is gravel) to the signed park entrance. There are two trailheads (upper and lower); hike directions begin at the lower trailhead. GPS (lower trailhead parking): N40 08.856' / W105 18.010'

# The Hike

Though Heil Valley Ranch is just one hogback ridge west of the high plains, it has a surprising alpine feel. Hiking through the fragrant ponderosa woodlands and pristine mountain meadows on the interpretive Lichen Loop, you might be convinced that you are much higher, and much farther removed from civilization, than you really are.

On the upper portions of the route, views open down and south along the Front Range toward Boulder, and there's no mistaking the park's location in the cleft in the hogback. The arid east-facing slopes of the mountain front rise to the west. Yucca and barrel cactus, plants more commonly found on the flatlands, dot the forest floor below the canopy of vanilla-scented ponderosas.

Heil Valley Ranch, neighboring Hall Ranch, and adjacent conservation easements make up an extensive wildlife habitat in the northern foothills. A menagerie of mountain creatures call the park home: raptors and the ground-dwelling rodents they prey on, mountain lions, black bears, songbirds, and mule deer, to name a few. An elk herd, reintroduced to the area at the beginning of the twentieth century, migrates between winter feeding grounds in the lowlands and summer range in the Indian Peaks Wilderness.

The park's history is typical of Front Range open spaces. Once the site of Native American camps, the property was most notably used as ranchland, but portions were also quarried for sandstone in the late 1800s. Interpretive signs along the trail describe both the human and natural history of the land, including its interesting geology.

The well-signed hike begins in the park's picnic area, following a broad gravel track along a seasonal stream to

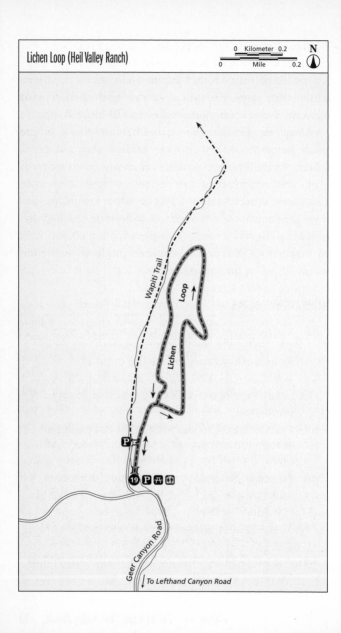

Lichen Loop (Heil Valley Ranch)

N

0    Kilometer    0.2

0         Mile         0.2

Wapiti Trail

Loop

Lichen

P

19  P

Geer Canyon Road

To Lefthand Canyon Road

the formal start of the loop, which is described here in a counterclockwise direction. Climb through a gently sloping meadow, then around the tail end of a small ridge into another sloping meadow. At the head of the second meadow, views open southward along the Front Range.

Above the meadows the trail enters the forest, where switchbacks weave through rocks colored with pale-green lichen. An interpretive sign describing ponderosa forests marks the beginning of the descent, which incorporates another set of switchbacks. In the meadow just before you close the loop, a side trail cuts a half-moon through the grasses and wildflowers to a kiva-like structure built of slabs of red rock. Once you've completed the loop, bear right and retrace your steps to the trailhead.

## Miles and Directions

**0.0** Start by crossing the bridge to the gravel trail on the right side of the stream. A sign notes that the trail's steward is *Backpacker* magazine. Picnic sites are on the left.

**0.1** At the second bridge (with an information kiosk and access to the parking lot and Wapiti Trail), go right on the signed Lichen Loop.

**0.2** Reach the start of the loop portion of the trail, just beyond an interpretive sign. Go right to make a counterclockwise circuit.

**0.6** Reach a second interpretive sign on geology at the top of the second meadow. Take in the views, then switchback up onto a wooded slope.

**0.8** A bench and interpretive sign mark another viewpoint. The switchbacking descent through ponderosa forest begins.

**1.0** Pass a blocked trail link to the Wapiti Trail, continuing left on the signed Lichen Loop.

**1.3** Take the short side trail that leads to the kiva-like red-rock enclosure.

**1.4** Close the loop; turn right and retrace your steps toward the trailhead.

**1.6** Arrive back at the trailhead.

## Options

The 2-mile out-and-back Little Thompson Overlook Trail, located in Rabbit Mountain Open Space Park (about 15 miles north of downtown Boulder and 2 miles east of Lyons), traverses high-desert scrub country to an overlook of the Little Thompson River canyon. The terrain is rugged and remote, hearkening back to the wild west.

# About the Author

Tracy Salcedo-Chourré has written more than twenty-five guidebooks to destinations in California and Colorado, including *Hiking Lassen Volcanic National Park, Exploring California's Missions and Presidios, Exploring Point Reyes National Seashore and the Golden Gate National Recreation Area, Best Rail Trails California,* and Best Easy Day Hikes guides to Boulder, Denver, Aspen, Colorado Springs, the San Francisco Bay Area, Lake Tahoe, Reno, and Sacramento.

Tracy is also an editor, teacher, and mom—but somehow still finds time to hike, swim, and garden. She lives with her husband, three sons, and a small menagerie of pets in California's Wine Country.

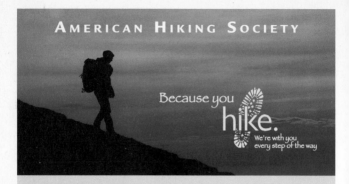